STORY SPARKERS:

A Creativity Guide for Children's Writers

We've been granted an interview with two of America's most successful children's writers. We get to hear how they started writing, what makes any story come to life, an astounding array of "sparkers," and the big and awesome secret behind publication.

Grab a cup of coffee, draw up a chair and go one on one with the message of hope that permeates this informative book. Thank God for Jones and Dadey and their logical, user-friendly, informative book on how to write for children. They've thought of everything.

—Jerrie Oughton, author of
How the Stars Fell Into the Sky: A Navajo Legend,
Perfect Family and *Music From a Place Called Half Moon*

STORY SPARKERS

A Creativity Guide for
Children's Writers

DEBBIE DADEY & MARCIA THORNTON JONES

authors of **The Adventures of the Bailey School Kids** series

Cincinnati, Ohio
www.writersdigest.com

Visit our Web site at www.writersdigest.com for information on more resources for writers.

To receive a free weekly E-mail newsletter delivering tips and updates about writing and about Writer's Digest products, send an E-mail with the message "Subscribe Newsletter" to newsletter-request@writersdigest.com or register directly at our Web site at www.writersdigest.com.

04 03 02 01 00   5 4 3 2 1

Library of Congress Cataloging-in-Publication Data

Jones, Marcia (Marcia Thornton)
   Story sparkers: a creativity guide for children's writers / by Marcia Thornton Jones and Debbie Dadey
      p. cm.
   title: Story sparkers
   Includes index.
   ISBN 1-58297-019-X (pbk.: alk. paper)
   1. Children's literature—Authorship. I. Title: Story sparkers. II. Dadey, Debbie. III. Title.

PN147.5. J67   2000
808.06′8—dc21   00-042250
                                                          CIP

Edited by Michelle Howry
Interior design by Matthew S. Gaynor
Production coordinated by Mark Griffin

ABOUT THE AUTHORS

The writers behind the best-selling Adventures of the Bailey School Kids series have something in common with the grown-ups who work at the Bailey School. No, Debbie Dadey and Marcia Thornton Jones are not vampires, elves, or even werewolves, but these authors were once teachers in the same elementary school in Lexington, Kentucky. Marcia was a reading teacher and Debbie was the head librarian when they decided they wanted to write for children. The two wrote every day while their students were eating lunch. But one fateful (and frustrating) day changed the direction of their stories forever. The kids were acting as if they had spring fever, so Marcia and Debbie figured they would have to sprout horns, blow smoke out of their noses, and grow ten feet tall to get the kids to pay attention! The idea made them laugh, so they decided to write a story about a teacher who might be a monster. That first book, *Vampires Don't Wear Polka Dots*, grew into the Adventures of the Bailey School Kids series.

The success of the Bailey School Kids has led Jones and Dadey to two more series, both published by Scholastic: Triplet Trouble (eight titles) and The Bailey City Monsters (three titles). Jones is the author of the top-selling *Godzilla Ate My Homework*, while Dadey is the author of *My Mom the Frog*. Both speak at writers conferences across the country. They also have a popular Web site: www.baileykids.com.

Debbie lives in Illinois, where she is full-time writer and mom. Marcia continues to teach in Lexington, KY.

CONTENTS

INTRODUCTION
Writers Don't Run Out of Ideas   1

CHAPTER 1
Get Sparking   5
How to Use This Book   5
Where to Write   6
The Markets   8
     Magazines
     Picture Books
     Easy Readers
     Chapter Books
     Middle-Grade Novels
     Young-Adult Novels
     Nonfiction
     Poetry and Verse

Which Genre Should *You* Choose?   20
What's Hot   21
What's Good   25
Summary   27

CHAPTER 2
The Blank Page   29
Brainstorming   31
Webbing   33
Freewriting   35
Listing   37
Questioning   38
Researching   39
The Five Senses   40
Overheard Conversations   42
Dialogues   43
Letters   44
     Real Letters
     Fictional Letters

The Big Idea   47
What If?   48
Thinking Small   49
Pictures   51
Pet Peeves   51
Reading   52
Forced Relationships   53
Time Lines   55
Possessions   57
Doodling   58
In My Shoes   59
Musical Muse   60
Summary   61

CHAPTER 3
A Famous Author Once Said . . .   63
Experiences and Memories   64
The Great Big World   66
Things Kids Care About   68
The School Connection
   (Curriculum-Based Ideas)   69
Writing to Remember   71
Where Did They Get Their Ideas?   72
Editors' Advice   87
Summary   88

CHAPTER 4
Igniting the Sparks   89
Fiction Elements   90
     Character
     Character Activities
     Setting
     Conflict
     Story Climax
     Resolution
     Plot

Nonfiction Elements   101
     Nonfiction Beginnings
     Nonfiction Middles
     Nonfiction Endings

Summary   106

CHAPTER 5
The Writing Process   107
Thinking   107
Drafting   109
Rewriting   110
Editing   114
Publishing   115
Our Writing Process   117
Summary   118

CHAPTER 6
Sculpting Your Ideas   119
Point of View   120
     First Person
     Third Person
     Third-Person Omniscient

Third-Person Limited Omniscient
Third-Person Objective

Voice — 123
Word Choice (or the Art of
  Being Specific) — 125
  Verbs and Adverbs
  Present Tense vs. Past Tense
  Active Verbs vs. Passive Verbs
  Verb Choice
  Adverbs
  Nouns and Adjectives
  Noun Choice
  Adjectives

Rhythm — 129
  Rhythm in Poetry and Verse

Hooks — 131
One-line Summary — 133
Theme — 134
Dialogue — 135
Show, Don't Tell — 137
Figurative Language — 137
  Metaphor
  Simile

Summary — 138

CHAPTER 7

A Firm Foundation — 141
Outlines — 141
Listing — 143
Subtopic — 143
Synopses of Sections — 144
Story Elements — 144
Plot Events — 146
Fiction-Book Planners — 146
Assessing Audience and
  Appropriate Genres — 149
Summary — 151

CHAPTER 8

When Your Battery Dies — 153
Writing Through Writer's Block — 153
Research to Enrich Ideas — 154
Write Out of Sequence — 156
Give Yourself Permission to Fail — 156
Recognize Your Distractions and
  Excuses — 157
Set Page or Word Quotas — 158

Enroll in a Writing Class or Workshop — 159
Collaborate With a Friend — 160
Join a Writers Group — 161
Read a Classic — 165
Review the Previous Day's Work — 166
Write a Letter to Your Audience — 167
Keep an Open Mind — 167
Set Attainable Goals — 168
Summary — 169

CHAPTER 9

A Leap of Faith — 171
Castles, Gazebos, and Mudrooms — 171
Golden Opportunities — 174
Panning for Gold: Choosing the
  Ideas to Pursue — 176
Jump In! — 179
Preparing Manuscripts — 179
Keeping Up With It All — 181
Summary — 183

APPENDICES

Appendix A: Awards and Honors — 187
Appendix B: Organizations — 188
Appendix C: Books — 188
Appendix D: Publications — 190
Appendix E: Web Sites — 190
Appendix F: Writer's Lingo — 191
Appendix G: Planners — 193
Appendix H: 100 Quick Story Sparks — 204

INDEX — 209

Hey kids look at this!

INTRODUCTION

Writers Don't Run Out of Ideas

"Don't you ever run out of ideas?" the girl with pigtails in the back of the room asked.

"Never!" we told her. "The only thing we run out of is time!"

It wasn't the first time we've heard that question. We were talking to a group of second-grade students in Kansas, but it doesn't seem to matter where we are or how old the audience is. Somebody always asks, "Don't you run out of ideas?"

The answer is always the same. "NO!"

We really mean it. Between the two of us we have published over seventy-five books in only nine years. That includes picture books, chapter books, a novel and five series including the best-selling Adventures of the Bailey School Kids series. And we've written even more stories that haven't found a publisher—yet! Our problem isn't running out of ideas . . . it's running out of *time* to pursue all the ideas we have!

Ideas are everywhere. They are walking down the sidewalk, hidden in stolen snippets of conversation, buried in the books we read and the movies we watch. Every waking minute—and every dreaming minute—is filled with tiny sparks just waiting to be ignited.

"Sure," you may be thinking. "It's easy for them to say. They're professional writers. They already know what they're doing."

If it could only be that easy! The truth is, we are professional writers, but only because we chose to be writers. Nobody taught us to write. Nobody guided us to this path. It was a conscious decision.

In fact, neither one of us considered writing for a possible career as we were growing up. We never had teachers show us how to write. We didn't think writers could be normal people like us. We thought great writers lived bohemian lives in Greenwich Village—or were already dead. The only writing we knew was the kind of writing that got us through college: term papers. And those weren't always easy!

But we made it through college and started our careers as elementary teachers. That's when we met. We were teachers in the same elementary school in Lexington, Kentucky. Debbie was the head librarian and Marcia was a reading teacher when we decided we wanted to write for children. Both of us loved reading, and we enjoyed using books to teach our students. We started talking about the great kids' books we read, comparing favorite authors. Having our names on a much-loved children's book sounded like it would be a great honor. Suddenly, Debbie stopped talking and looked at Marcia. "What's stopping us from trying to write a children's book?" Debbie asked.

Marcia thought, and she thought hard. But the truth is, there was no reason not to try. So that's just what we did. The next day we started writing during our twenty-minute teachers' lunch break.

We had a lot to learn. We wrote every day, took writing courses, attended conferences, and did extensive research. We thought there were "rules" for success that everybody else knew and was keeping secret from us. But we found only one true rule for success in this business (and it is a business), and we're willing to share it with you.

If you want to be a writer, you have to come up with clever ideas worth developing and actually write them. So we wrote, and we wrote a lot.

For two years we studied, researched, and wrote . . . but with very little success. One fateful (and frustrating) day changed the direction of our stories. The kids in Marcia's classroom had spring fever. They wouldn't listen, they weren't doing their work, and they were downright rude. We decided we would have to sprout horns, blow smoke out our noses, and grow ten feet tall just to get the kids to pay attention! The idea made us laugh so we decided to write a story about a teacher who just might be a monster. That first book, *Vampires Don't Wear Polka Dots*, grew into The Adventures of the Bailey School Kids series.

Good for them, you may be thinking. But what about writers who aren't teachers, writers who don't have the serendipitous opportunities found in a classroom setting?

Don't worry. By the time you finish reading this book, you will understand that sparks of ideas for children's books are everywhere, just waiting for you to discover them and start writing!

GET SPARKING

How to Use This Book

Sparks are tiny glowing embers capable of igniting into a brilliant fire—or of being completely snuffed out by the surrounding ash.

As writers, we need to discover our own buried story sparks capable of igniting into full-fledged stories, articles, and poems. The strategies and exercises in this book will help you dig through the ash and find those glowing embers that will spark your writing, igniting it until it glows.

Writing is a creative process, unique to each individual. This book is designed to help you get your ideas and words flowing. While this book is intended for novice writers interested in writing for the children's market, experienced writers will find it inspirational and motivating, too.

Chapter 1 provides a brief introduction to the different genres that make up the children's market. The brainstorming activities in chapter 2 offer many strategies that will help you get started from scratch. Chapter 3 shows you how successful writers make the idea-generating strategies work for them. A review of the fiction and nonfiction elements in chapter 4 and of the writing process in chapter 5 will equip you with fundamental writing tools. Chapter 6 touches on a potpourri of important concepts such as point of view, voice, and dialogue. Chapter 7 will help you focus your search for ideas to develop throughout your writing pieces. The strategies in chapter 8 will help you stay motivated, even when you feel your inspiration sputtering. Chapter 9 puts it all together and gives you a systematic process for starting your writing life. Each chapter includes activities that help illustrate these strategies and spark your writing.

Since this book is intended to get you writing, you will have to make one decision before you go any farther. Where will you write down all the ideas you generate?

Where to Write

The "Try It Yourself" exercises in this book are designed to capture your great ideas and get them down on paper. Before reading farther, we recommend you decide how and where to store all your ideas.

Marcia likes using bound journals for collecting ideas. Journals aren't expensive; you can usually find them on a sale table at most bookstores (but Marcia never has to buy one; she always ends up getting several lovely ones for Christmas and birthday presents). She likes the idea of a bound book because it allows her to maintain a personal record of her writing progress. Seeing where and when ideas seem to flow and where they are sparse gives her an idea of how her writing is developing. Marcia prefers journals without lines. According to her, the flow of ideas doesn't happen in a linear fashion, so why have those lines stretching so neatly across the page? If she feels like starting in the middle of a page and allowing her writing to radiate in concentric circles, those lines would just get in the way! The first few pages of each journal includes a table of contents where she notes the date each entry was made, the main idea of the entries, and whether or not an entry is a possible story idea. The table of contents provides a quick reference in case she needs to find an idea to develop in the future.

Some writers don't care for the "permanence" of a bound journal. If that's you, you might want to try jotting ideas on loose-leaf paper or in a spiral notebook. Spiral notebooks can be found at a minimal cost, and their flexible covers and spiral binding make them easy to use. Loose-leaf paper gives you the ultimate in portability. A few pieces of paper are easily folded and stuffed in your purse or pocket, ready to be pulled out when inspiration strikes.

Of course, some writers rely on computers. Computers are wonderful tools that allow you to concentrate on *ideas* instead of on handwriting. If that sounds appealing to you, you may want to dedicate a file for ideas.

TRY IT YOURSELF

1. Where will you store your story sparks from this book? If you plan to use a new journal, go buy one! If you would rather enter your ideas into the computer, dedicate a file for your sparks right now. If you're going to jot down your sparks on napkins and toilet paper and throw them in a box, find a box and get it ready!
2. Look through the Table of Contents of this book. Make a plan for working through the contents.
3. Give yourself permission to invest valuable time sparking your writing.

Maybe you're more like Debbie and end up writing on notepads, napkins, the backs of canceled checks, or even toilet paper rolls. If that works for you, then do it. Putting everything in a shoe box or file folder labeled *Ideas* will give you a place to turn when you're ready for a new story.

Whether you use scraps of paper, index cards, your computer, or bound notebooks, it's a good idea to keep your writing materials handy—you never know when a good idea will demand to be written. And do write down the ideas when they come to you. It's easy to fall victim to the belief that you'll remember your ideas later, but that isn't always the case. Leonardo da Vinci kept one or two notebooks chained to his belt at all times. Debbie's husband complains about the notepads she has scattered all over the house. (But he's never complained once about her royalty checks!)

Whatever method you use to store your wealth of ideas, never throw anything away. Even if you think your work is worthless, horrible, and clichéd don't throw it away. Sometimes those false starts and bad ideas just need time to ferment. Picture-book author W. Nikola-Lisa often carries an idea around for years until it ripens or an external event pulls it to the front of his attention. So whether it's in a journal, a notebook, a file folder, a big box that you throw ideas into, or a combination of them all, remember to save everything! This will become your system for maintaining a personal record of your creative process.

One more very important thing we need to mention about the "Try It Yourself" exercises in this book: There are no wrong answers! If an exercise results in writing you don't like, don't worry about it. Nothing you write is forever. You always have the option of changing it or starting over or just moving on. Your responses are for your eyes only—unless, of course, you choose to show them to someone else. That means the exercises in this book are risk-free! Let's take a look at the exercises on page 7 and get started right away!

The Markets

There are abundant opportunities for writers of children's literature. Readers of children's books range from toddler to young adult. That means there is a market for a wide range of topics, styles, and genres. You just have to figure out which best suits your writing and the ideas you write about. What follows is a look at the different types of children's markets.

THE CHILDREN'S MARKET		
Genre	**Intended Audience**	**Manuscript Length (in double-spaced typed pages)**
Picture Book	toddler–grade 4	2–10
Easy Reader/Beginning Chapter Book	grades K–3	15–25
Young Chapter Book	grades 2–4	30–50
Middle-Grade Novels	grades 3–7	60–150
Young-Adult Novels	grades 8–12	150–300
Magazine	toddler–grade 12	1–5
Nonfiction	toddler–grade 12	2–300
Poetry	toddler–grade 12	1

Magazines

You may find magazines to be the perfect market for your short stories, poetry, and nonfiction articles. Publishing your work in magazines helps build your writing credentials and establishes you as a professional writer. Magazines are a great place to publish poetry and verse, puzzles, fiction, and nonfiction (including how-to articles). Editors of children's magazines look for timely pieces aimed at children growing up in today's fast-paced society. Books can take years to hit the market, a once-timely topic long since forgotten by the time a book hits the shelves. Magazines, on the other hand, can be in a reader's hands in just a matter of months. Especially suited to the magazine market are writing pieces focusing on current events, problems, and issues.

Magazines also provide a market for your specialized projects that would otherwise have a limited audience. Most magazines limit their focus to a specific content. Cheerleading, for example, is the central focus of *American Cheerleader*; *Calliope*'s is dedicated to history; and *Dolphin Log* is devoted to marine ecology and its environment.

Magazines aren't only limited in their content. The intended audiences of most periodicals are limited to particular age levels and genders. *Babybug*'s intended audience is toddlers while the *Keynoter* is aimed at high school students. *Boys' Life* is geared to boys and *Hopscotch* is a magazine for girls.

You might find magazines perfect for breaking into the writing market. Be sure to become thoroughly familiar with a magazine before trying to market your work to it. It's always a good idea to read several issues and to write for the publisher's guidelines; some magazines (like *Cobblestone*) devote entire issues to a focused topic or theme. Also keep in mind that magazines often purchase pieces well ahead of time—some even buy copy a year in advance—so plan ahead.

Puzzles, poems, and article ideas that are focused and can be developed in fewer than 1,000 words might be suited for the magazine market. Author/illustrator Paul Brett Johnson also recommends considering this market for your short fiction pieces in which the words tell the whole story. "If the words tell the whole story," he told us, "it's not a picture book. It belongs in a magazine." But if your fiction piece could be enhanced by illustrations, read on!

Picture Books

Chances are, when you think of children's books you think of picture books. Picture books are beautifully illustrated books targeted for readers from toddler to grade four. But, keep in mind that the picture book idea must also appeal to adults, since they usually shell out the money for these expensive books.

Picture books can cover a wide range of subjects. They include fiction like *The Longest Wait* by Marie Bradby and nonfiction stories such as *If You Were Born a Kitten* by Marion Dane Bauer. Picture books may be about animals that act like animals as in *A Traveling Cat* by George Ella Lyon, animals that act like people as in the *Little Bear* books by Else Holmelund Minarik, or about people interacting with people as in Mem Fox's *Wilfrid Gordon McDonald Partridge*. Retellings of fairy tales, tall tales, and legends such as Paul Zelinsky's *Rapunzel*, Debbie Dadey's *Shooting Star: Annie Oakley, the Legend*, and Jerrie Oughton's *How the Stars Fell Into the Sky: A Navajo Legend*, often appear as picture books, too. The possibilities of picture books are limitless as long as the ideas are fresh and exciting.

Picture books are typically thirty-two pages, and that includes the copyright and title pages, called "front matter." The actual story may only be twenty-eight pages. If the book is formatted to include double spreads where the picture works with the text across the two pages of the open book, the story must be told in fourteen pages. As you can see, the picture book writer has to pack a big punch in very few words. The manuscript of a picture book is generally less than 2,000 words. Most are under 1,000 words.

There is a misconception that many writers "start" by writing picture books before moving on to longer pieces. This is not remotely true. Just because picture books are short doesn't mean they're easy to write. In fact, the brevity of picture books makes them one of the most difficult stories to write and sell. Every word, phrase, and scene must count in a picture book. There is no room for unnecessary details or subplots. Picture books must be finely crafted.

Even though the picture book's intended audience is young, don't feel constrained by simplistic vocabulary and sentence structure. Keep in mind that picture books are meant to be read *to* young children, not read *by* them. A strong writer's voice that is easily heard in oral readings enhances the picture-book story. And don't fall into the thinking trap that all picture books rhyme. Rhyming stories remain favorites for young readers, but they're extremely difficult to write well. Rather than thinking in rhyme, try using prose that shows your picture-book story unfolding in natural, vibrant language. If your story can be told in prose, then do it and leave the rhyming to somebody else.

Unfortunately, editors are also inundated with manuscripts that are stale, clichéd, and poorly crafted. At one writers' conference we sank deeper and deeper in our chairs as we listened to an editor recite clichéd ideas. The poor little Christmas tree that no one would choose? We did that. The rabbit with ears too long? Ours was the giraffe whose neck was too long. The unwanted pet saves the day, or maybe it was all just a dream? Done it!

Don't get us wrong. These aren't bad ideas. They're just so good that they've been written about—over and over and over again until they've become clichés. Approach your ideas in a fresh and exciting way. Give an idea a new twist that makes an editor, parent, and most importantly, a child, sit up and want to read!

You may be thinking, *But I can't draw, so there is no way I could write for children.* The good news is the picture-book writer doesn't have to worry about producing the pictures. Most editors prefer to see picture-book manuscripts without any reference to illustrations. Editors want your story to stand on its own merit. When an editor decides to publish your manuscript, he or she will select an illustrator to make your story come alive through art.

Writers of picture books need to consider more than the words of their story. They must also think visually: Consider how the story can be shown through pictures varied enough to fill fourteen to twenty-eight pages.

Ask yourself if your idea is suited for a young audience and can support enough scene changes for fourteen to twenty-eight illustrations. We once wrote about the possibility of a monster under the bed. We thought it was a great story, but the visuals were limited to under the bed in the middle of the night—rather hard to illustrate!

In short, a fresh idea that can be told in less than 2,000 words and lends itself to fourteen to eighteen illustrations will work for the picture-book market. Your completed manuscript will range between two and ten double-spaced pages. If the story isn't enhanced in some way by the illustrations, it may be better suited for the magazine market.

A great way to assimilate the language, pacing, and plotting of picture-book stories is to examine books that have been awarded the Caldecott Medal. The Association of Library Service to Children, a division of the American Library Association, presents this award annually to a picture-book artist.

CALDECOTT MEDAL BOOKS

Year	Title	Author	Illustrator
2000	Joseph Had a Little Overcoat	Simms Taback	Simms Taback
1999	Snowflake Bentley	Jacqueline Briggs Martin	Mary Azarian
1998	Rapunzel	Paul O. Zelinsky	Paul O. Zelinsky
1997	Golem	David Wisniewski	David Wisniewski
1996	Officer Buckle and Gloria	Peggy Rathmann	Peggy Rathmann
1995	Smoky Night	Eve Bunting	David Diaz
1994	Grandfather's Journey	Allen Say	Allen Say
1993	Mirette on the High Wire	Emily Arnold McCully	Emily Arnold McCully
1992	Tuesday	David Wiesner	David Wiesner
1991	Black and White	David Macaulay	David Macaulay
1990	Lon Po Po: A Red-Riding Hood Story From China	Ed Young	Ed Young
1989	Song and Dance Man	Karen Ackerman	Stephen Gammell
1988	Owl Moon	Jane Yolen	John Schoenherr
1987	Hey, Al	Arthur Yorinks	Richard Egielski

CALDECOTT MEDAL BOOKS

Year	Title	Author	Illustrator
1986	The Polar Express	Chris Van Allsburg	Chris Van Allsburg
1985	Saint George and the Dragon	Margaret Hodges	Trina Schart Hyman
1984	The Glorious Flight: Across the Channel with Louis Blériot	Alice and Martin Provensen	Alice and Martin Provensen
1983	Shadow (written by Blaise Cendrars)	Translated by Marcia Brown	Marcia Brown
1982	Jumanji	Chris Van Allsburg	Chris Van Allsburg
1981	Fables	Arnold Lobel	Arnold Lobel
1980	Ox-Cart Man	Donald Hall	Barbara Cooney
1979	The Girl Who Loved Wild Horses	Paul Goble	Paul Goble
1978	Noah's Ark	Peter Spier	Peter Spier
1977	Ashanti to Zulu: African Traditions	Margaret Musgrove	Leo and Diane Dillon
1976	Why Mosquitoes Buzz in People's Ears: A West African Tale	Verna Aardema	Leo and Diane Dillon
1975	Arrow to the Sun	Gerald McDermott	Gerald McDermott
1974	Duffy and the Devil	Harve and Margot Zemach	Harve and Margot Zemach
1973	The Funny Little Woman	Arlene Mosel	Blair Lent
1972	One Fine Day	Nonny Hogrogian	Nonny Hogrogian
1971	A Story, a Story	Gail E. Haley	Gail E. Haley
1970	Sylvester and the Magic Pebble	William Steig	William Steig
1969	The Fool of the World and the Flying Ship	Arthur Ransome	Uri Shulevitz
1968	Drummer Hoff	Barbara Emberley	Ed Emberley
1967	Sam, Bangs, and Moonshine	Evaline Ness	Evaline Ness
1966	Always Room for One More	Sorche Nic Leodhas	Nonny Hogrogian
1965	May I Bring a Friend?	Beatrice Schenk de Regniers	Beni Montresor
1964	Where the Wild Things Are	Maurice Sendak	Maurice Sendak
1963	The Snowy Day	Ezra Jack Keats	Ezra Jack Keats
1962	Once a Mouse	Marcia Brown	Marcia Brown
1961	Baboushka and the Three Kings	Ruth Robbins	Nicolas Sidjakov
1960	Nine Days to Christmas: A Story of Mexico	Marie Hall Ets and Aurora Labastida	Marie Hall Ets and Aurora Labastida
1959	Chanticleer and the Fox (adapted from Chaucer's Canterbury Tales)	Adapted by Barbara Cooney	Barbara Cooney
1958	Time of Wonder	Robert McCloskey	Robert McCloskey
1957	A Tree Is Nice	Janice May Udry	Marc Simont
1956	Frog Went A-Courtin'	John Langstaff	Feodor Rojankovsky
1955	Cinderella (written by Charles Perrault)	Translated by Marcia Brown	Marcia Brown
1954	Madeline's Rescue	Ludwig Bemelmans	Ludwig Bemelmans
1953	The Biggest Bear	Lynd Ward	Lynd Ward
1952	Finders Keepers	William Lipkind and Nicolas Mordvinoff	Nicolas Mordvinoff
1951	The Egg Tree	Katherine Milhous	Katherine Milhous
1950	Song of the Swallows	Leo Politi	Leo Politi
1949	The Big Snow	Berta and Elmer Hader	Berta and Elmer Hader
1948	White Snow, Bright Snow	Alvin Tresselt	Roger Duvoisin

CALDECOTT MEDAL BOOKS

Year	Title	Author	Illustrator
1947	The Little Island	Golden MacDonald (Margaret Wise Brown)	Leonard Weisgard
1946	The Rooster Crows: A Book of American Rhymes and Jingles	Maud and Miska Petersham	Maud and Miska Petersham
1945	Prayer for a Child	Rachel Field	Elizabeth Orton Jones
1944	Many Moons	James Thurber	Louis Slobodkin
1943	The Little House	Virginia Lee Burton	Virginia Lee Burton
1942	Make Way for Ducklings	Robert McCloskey	Robert McCloskey
1941	They Were Strong and Good	Robert Lawson	Robert Lawson
1940	Abraham Lincoln	Ingri and Edgar Parin d'Aulaire	Ingri and Edgar Parin d'Aulaire
1939	Mei Li	Thomas Handforth	Thomas Handforth
1938	Animals of the Bible	Helen Dean Fish	Dorothy Lathrop

Easy Readers

"I don't want a baby book," a first grader says. Librarians, teachers, and parents often hear beginning readers say this. Of course they don't! They've spent hours struggling to learn the written language and now they want to show off a little. Who can blame them? Do you remember looking at those "fat" books that older kids always checked out? Wishing you could be "big" enough to read them but not yet possessing the necessary reading skills? Easy readers are for kids at that in-between stage—an imperative time in a young reader's development. It's easy to lose a reader whose developing skills make longer, more complex works frustrating. That's where easy readers come in: If you can hook that same young reader with a good story that he can conquer, then you have a reader for life!

Easy readers are intended as a step up from the picture book for kids in kindergarten through third grade, though adults are still the primary purchasers. The book format is narrower and taller to look like longer works of fiction. The published story is often divided into sections that resemble chapters and tend to run about sixty-four pages long.

Easy readers rely on simple illustrations to break up the text and promote understanding, but illustrations aren't as important as they are in picture books. The plot is kept simple by focusing on one main event and one character. It's important to make sure the characters are kids and that a child protagonist solves the conflict. Kids this age will read cross-gender; boys don't seem to mind reading about a girl protagonist and the same goes for girls. Humor, suspense, and action keep the plots moving in these fast-paced stories, and page-turning hooks are necessary to keep your readers enthusiastic. Easy readers open a whole world of topics. Kids have just started the school scene, and they are becoming more aware of nature, family relationships, competitiveness, and their own emotions. Readers at this age level enjoy the predictability of books series like the Frog and Toad books by Arnold Lobel, Marjorie Sharmat's Nate the Great books, and Peggy Parish's Amelia Bedelia stories.

Dialogue is used freely in easy readers for two reasons: Dialogue is an effective way to move the plot, and it helps provide lots of "white space" on the page, making it easier for beginning readers to conquer a page. Sentence structure is natural but kept simple. Don't worry about using a specified vocabulary list. Readers of this age use context clues to decode new words, so make sure the meaning of complicated language can be determined by the story content.

If you're thinking about developing an idea for this audience, make the plot simple and keep the cast limited to one or two major characters. Your completed manuscript will run between fifteen and twenty-five double-spaced pages.

Chapter Books

Chapter books are written for first through fourth graders—readers who are reading independently, but are still not ready for longer, more traditional novels. Readers of this age are starting to make their own decisions and have an allowance to back them up, so they are the primary purchasers. However, schools are relying more and more on trade books to supplement their reading curriculum, so teachers are always looking for appropriate chapter books to use in the classroom.

Kids at this age want to read about characters that are like them, who are their age or a little older. They generally don't like reading about characters younger than themselves. Boys tend to choose books with strong male characters, and girls would rather read stories about strong female characters. In both cases, the story should revolve around a child protagonist in a kid-centered setting, with the conflict being resolved by kids, not adults. In fact, some books don't even have adult characters in them; readers want to see *kids* as heroes. These books are definitely written about a child's world.

Like easy readers, chapter books include many short chapters, but they do not rely as heavily on illustrations as do easy readers. The chapter-book story must stand alone, without the aid of illustrations. Most illustrations for this level are simple black-and-white drawings.

Text appears more densely on the page than in the easy reader, but plenty of dialogue still helps move the plot. The stories tend to be fast-paced and may include more complicated plots and a small cast of characters. But the readers of these books can handle a more serious and in-depth story, too. Historical fiction, humor, mystery, and action stories are popular. Favorite themes involve school, relationships, animals, family, and friends. Kids are great collectors at this age, which helps explain the popularity of series books. But, just as with the easy readers, readers like the predictability found in a series.

Chapter books can accommodate a variety of sentence structures and can allow for more complicated vocabulary, making the written language flow. Strive for natural language.

This is the genre we write for. Marcia's *Godzilla Ate My Homework*, Debbie's *My Mom the Frog*, and two of our series are aimed for these readers. E.B. White's *Charlotte's Web* is an all-time favorite, along with all of Beverly Cleary's books including *Henry Huggins*, *Ribsy*, and the Ramona titles. Two other popular chapter-book series are Mary Pope Osborne's Magic Tree House series and the American Girls series.

Chapter-book manuscripts usually run between thirty and fifty double-spaced pages.

Middle-Grade Novels

Middle-grade novels are written for an older audience—readers in grades three through seven. Plots are often more complex than chapter books and are usually built around issues that students of this age are concerned with, including family and peer relationships. Of course, school is the biggest focus for readers in this age group, so many middle-grade novels revolve around school issues.

Plot lines and characters are much more developed in this category, and there is room for subtle subplots. Illustrations are rarely seen, and there isn't as much "white space" on the pages. Dialogue is still important, but there is room for more description. The language is fresh, honest, and natural. Don't mistake that to mean middle-grade novels are littered with slang; that's almost never the case. It's tempting to use the current vernacular of today's youth while writing, but it could take your book a year or two to hit the shelves once it's accepted. By that time new buzzwords could be circling the halls of the middle schools, making your story sound dated and obsolete. Make your story timeless by avoiding slang when possible.

Idea possibilities are unlimited for novels. Readers in this age group like fantasy stories like the Harry Potter books by J.K. Rowling, mysteries like Donald J. Sobol's Encyclopedia Brown series, humorous stories such as *Crash* by Jerry Spinelli, and historical books like Debbie Dadey's *Cherokee Sister*. Judy Blume showed how important it is to write with honesty about kid concerns with her popular books, including *Are You There God? It's Me, Margaret*. R.L. Stine proved that series are still popular at this level with the phenomenal success of his Goosebumps series. One interesting thing to note: Many books intended for middle-grade readers are being read by younger audiences, too. Even though Goosebumps was meant for an older audience, they wound up in the hands of capable first graders.

In novels, chapters are longer and sentence structure can be complex. Manuscripts usually range from one hundred to three hundred pages long.

An excellent source for highly acclaimed middle-grade novels is the list of Newbery Medal winners. The Association for Library Service to Children, a division of the American Library Association, awards this annual honor. Most winning books fall into the novel category. Study the list of Newbery-winning novels on pages 17–18 to learn the plotting, characterizations, and style that make a novel really stand out.

Young-Adult Novels

Here is yet another type of book written for children, albeit older children from the ages of twelve to fifteen. Kids in middle school and high school are able to deal with serious themes that border on adult. Young-adult protagonists and plots are directly related to this age group. Problem books—stories whose plots focus on problems such as cancer, pregnancy, and eating disorders—were popular for a while. But for today's market it's better to incorporate social problems and issues into the development of a strong set of characters who appear to be dealing with their everyday lives. Coming-of-age, family, friends, relationships, and social issues are popular themes for these books.

Keep in mind that some of the readers in this age group are already experimenting with adult books, such as those written by Stephen King. That means you'll need to make the language and content on more of an adult level. Most kids, but especially readers in this category, will not sit still while being talked down to or preached at. You'll also find the use of adult language. Cursing can lend a sense of authenticity to a character's role, but don't use swearing gratuitously; be sure any off-color language serves a specific purpose.

The text in young-adult novels is similar to adult books, but chapters are a bit shorter. While subplots help make the plot richer, they probably

NEWBERY MEDAL WINNERS

Year	Title	Author
2000	Bud, Not Buddy	Christopher Paul Curtis
1999	Holes	Louis Sachar
1998	Out of the Dust	Karen Hesse
1997	The View From Saturday	E.L. Konigsburg
1996	The Midwife's Apprentice	Karen Cushman
1995	Walk Two Moons	Sharon Creech
1994	The Giver	Lois Lowry
1993	Missing May	Cynthia Rylant
1992	Shiloh	Phyllis Reynolds Naylor
1991	Maniac Magee	Jerry Spinelli
1990	Number the Stars	Lois Lowry
1989	Joyful Noise: Poems for Two Voices	Paul Fleischman
1988	Lincoln: A Photobiography	Russell Freedman
1987	The Whipping Boy	Sid Fleischman
1986	Sarah, Plain and Tall	Patricia MacLachlan
1985	The Hero and the Crown	Robin McKinley
1984	Dear Mr. Henshaw	Beverly Cleary
1983	Dicey's Song	Cynthia Voigt
1982	A Visit to William Blake's Inn: Poems for Innocent and Experienced Travelers	Nancy Willard
1981	Jacob Have I Loved	Katherine Paterson
1980	A Gathering of Days: A New England Girl's Journal	Joan W. Blos
1979	The Westing Game	Ellen Raskin
1978	Bridge to Terabithia	Katherine Paterson
1977	Roll of Thunder, Hear My Cry	Mildred D. Taylor
1976	The Grey King	Susan Cooper
1975	M. C. Higgins, the Great	Virginia Hamilton
1974	The Slave Dancer	Paula Fox
1973	Julie of the Wolves	Jean Craighead George
1972	Mrs. Frisby and the Rats of NIMH	Robert C. O'Brien
1971	The Summer of the Swans	Betsy Cromer Byars
1970	Sounder	William H. Armstrong
1969	The High King	Lloyd Alexander
1968	From the Mixed-Up Files of Mrs. Basil E. Frankweiler	E. L. Konigsburg
1967	Up a Road Slowly	Irene Hunt
1966	I, Juan de Pareja	Elizabeth Borton de Trevino
1965	Shadow of a Bull	Maia Wojciechowska
1964	It's Like This, Cat	Emily Neville
1963	A Wrinkle in Time	Madeleine L'Engle
1962	The Bronze Bow	Elizabeth George Speare
1961	Island of the Blue Dolphins	Scott O'Dell
1960	Onion John	Joseph Krumgold
1959	The Witch of Blackbird Pond	Elizabeth George Speare
1958	Rifles for Watie	Harold Keith

NEWBERY MEDAL WINNERS

Year	Title	Author
1957	Miracles on Maple Hill	Virginia Sorenson
1956	Carry On, Mr. Bowditch	Jean Lee Latham
1955	The Wheel on the School	Meindert DeJong
1954	. . . And Now Miguel	Joseph Krumgold
1953	Secret of the Andes	Ann Nolan Clark
1952	Ginger Pye	Eleanor Estes
1951	Amos Fortune, Free Man	Elizabeth Yates
1950	The Door in the Wall	Marguerite de Angeli
1949	King of the Wind	Marguerite Henry
1948	The Twenty-One Balloons	William Pène du Bois
1947	Miss Hickory	Carolyn Sherwin Bailey
1946	Strawberry Girl	Lois Lenski
1945	Rabbit Hill	Robert Lawson
1944	Johnny Tremain	Esther Forbes
1943	Adam of the Road	Elizabeth Janet Gray
1942	The Matchlock Gun	Walter Dumaux Edmonds
1941	Call It Courage	Armstrong Sperry
1940	Daniel Boone	James Daugherty
1939	Thimble Summer	Elizabeth Enright
1938	The White Stag	Kate Seredy
1937	Roller Skates	Ruth Sawyer
1936	Caddie Woodlawn	Carol Ryrie Brink
1935	Dobry	Monica Shannon
1934	Invincible Louisa: The Story of the Author of *Little Women*	Cornelia Meigs
1933	Young Fu of the Upper Yangtze	Elizabeth Foreman Lewis
1932	Waterless Mountain	Laura Adams Armer
1931	The Cat Who Went to Heaven	Elizabeth Coatsworth
1930	Hitty: Her First Hundred Years	Rachel Field
1929	The Trumpeter of Krakow	Eric P. Kelly
1928	Gay-Neck: The Story of a Pigeon	Dhan Gopal Mukerji
1927	Smoky the Cowhorse	Will James
1926	Shen of the Sea: Chinese Stories for Children	Arthur Bowie Chrisman
1925	Tales From the Silver Lands	Charles J. Finger
1924	The Dark Frigate	Charles Boardman Hawes
1923	The Voyages of Doctor Dolittle	Hugh Lofting
1922	The Story of Mankind	Hendrik Willem van Loon

aren't as deep as they are in adult novels. One major difference between the adult and young-adult novel is that stories for teenagers will revolve around characters in high school while adult books focus on adult protagonists.

Slam! by Walter Dean Myers, *The Pigman* by Paul Zindel, and Jerrie Oughton's *Music From a Place Called Half Moon* are excellent examples of this genre. Manuscripts range from 150 to 300 pages. The Michael L. Printz Award winners for young-adult literature are worth reviewing. The first Printz Award was given in 2000 to Walter Dean Myers for his novel, *Monster*.

Nonfiction

You only have to look at a few recently published children's nonfiction books to realize they have changed dramatically in the last twenty years. No longer dry, didactic sources of information, they are now written in a kid-friendly manner that almost reads like fiction. Nonfiction can be published for any book or magazine genre.

Nonfiction books can be aimed at any age. There are simply worded nonfiction picture books like Marion Dane Bauer's *If You Were Born a Kitten*, and chapter books that present more information but are still fairly easy to read like Jerry Spinelli's *Knots in My Yo-Yo String*. Then there are more in-depth sources—e.g., *Lincoln: A Photobiography* by Russell Freedman, *Lewis Hayden and the War Against Slavery* by Joel Strangis—that kids rely on for school reports and teachers use to supplement their curricula.

Nonfiction is not simply a recitation of facts learned during research. Well-written nonfiction employs the same stylistic writing techniques as fiction books to make the topic come alive for young readers. There is no room for preachy writing and lists of facts. You want the reader to feel a part of the nonfiction topic, so use techniques that draw the reader into the piece. Longer nonfiction works often include charts, tables, graphs, illustrations, photographs, glossaries, recommended reading lists, bibliographies, and footnotes. Manuscript lengths for nonfiction fall into the same categories as fiction.

Topics can cover anything that kids in your intended audience would be curious about. Animals and everyday objects are favorites of preschool readers, while monsters and sports remain popular for readers in elementary school. Older readers look for books that will help them succeed in their everyday lives and in their school projects.

Peruse the library and bookstores to see what's available and how these books are written as you develop your nonfiction ideas. Above all, make sure your reader is part of the story.

Poetry and Verse

Children love verse and poetry. This genre has enjoyed a resurgence in past years thanks to the poetry of Shel Silverstein, Lee Bennett Hopkins, and Jack Prelutsky.

Poetry and verse are often published as anthologies. These collections might be full of short fun-loving verse that's easy enough for a second grader, like Carol Diggory Shields's *Lunch Money and Other Poems about School*, or innovative poetry that's found in *Joyful Noise: Poems for Two Voices* by Paul Fleischman. They could also be comprised of the multilayered and complex poetry that appeals to young adults like those in *The Inner City Mother Goose* by Eve Merriam or *If I Were in Charge of the World and Other Worries: Poems for Children and Their Parents* by Judith Viorst.

The poetry and verse genre includes simple rhyming couplets; structured poetry such as limericks, cinquains, and sonnets; or verse that is free of meter and rhyme, known as "free verse." Poetry books can be lengthy compilations, but they may also contain only a few poems centered on a specific theme. In fact, a single poem or verse can stand on its own and be illustrated as a picture book, such as the heartwarming *When Mama Comes Home Tonight* by Eileen Spinelli.

Don't worry if you don't have a collection of poetry to market. Both magazine and book markets publish poetry. Magazines would be perfect for those one or two poems you'd like to publish. Poetry is published for all ages, so if you enjoy writing poetry and verse, you will be able to find an appropriate market.

As you can see, writing for children includes a wide range of potential markets. Sometimes, the lines can be fuzzy. Look at the phenomenal success of the Harry Potter books by J.K. Rowling. These books not only crossed over genre lines in the children's market, but they jumped to the adult best-seller list, too.

All this is good news for you. It means your ideas are bound to be appropriate for at least one level in this market! But how do you decide which genre to write for?

Which Genre Should *You* Choose?

We know what you're thinking: "All those genres! How will I ever know which one best suits my writing?"

If you spend too much time trying to figure out which genre best suits you, you may never get any of your ideas on paper. But some things may be pretty obvious. Answer these questions and you'll see what we mean.

⋆ Do you like to read nonfiction?
⋆ When you go to the library, do you search the shelves for fanciful fiction stories?

★ Are you drawn to the brevity of picture-book stories?

★ Are you the type who likes to leaf through magazines, reading short, focused articles?

★ Do you prefer the dreamy imagery and romping rhymes of poetry?

Our best advice to all writers is, don't try and fit your ideas into a box before they're even hatched. Instead, write the type of stories, articles, and poetry you enjoy reading. Marcia's husband once teased her by asking when she was going to "grow up enough to read adult-level books." The truth is, Marcia likes reading children's books. And those are the types of stories she enjoys writing.

After you've developed your ideas, you can determine which genre best suits your writing. Revising and editing will help shape the developed idea to fit the most appropriate market. If you still feel more comfortable thinking within the structure of a certain genre, then write the kinds of things you like to read.

What's Hot

People often try to write stories to fit a really "hot" publishing trend. The problem with that philosophy is that trends rapidly change; by the time you finish your story, a new trend may be driving the market. For a while, "problem" novels dealing with heavy social issues like cancer, AIDS, and eating disorders were popular for the young-adult market. While those topics are still worth writing about, they're not "hot" like they once were. Now they're more likely to be dealt with as part of a strong character or coming-of-age plot. Of course some trends stick around awhile. Multicultural books, mysteries, and fantasies have been popular for a long time and will probably continue to be in demand.

It can be helpful to study the current market. Identifying what's being published can only help make you a better writer and more effective at marketing your work. But instead of trying to shape your writing to fit a specific trend, concentrate on writing the best story you can.

If trends have changed in children's literature, does that mean kids have changed, too? We don't think so. Deep down, we think kids are still kids just like they were thirty, forty, fifty, even one hundred years ago. Sure, many kids are more worldly than kids of twenty years ago. We've met children who have traveled all over the world and think nothing of going to Africa or Paris during their spring vacations. Most kids today are used to instantaneous entertainment, thanks to the television and video games. In our country particularly, many kids are used to having what they want and having it now. But they still want friends

TRY IT YOURSELF

1. Identify the kinds of books you like to read. Go to the library and sample poetry, magazines, picture books, easy readers, middle-grade fiction, young-adult novels, and nonfiction books. The list on pages 23–25 will help you locate excellent examples of each genre. It is only a sampling of some of our favorites and is by no means exhaustive.

   Then find your own current favorites. (To discover current publishing trends, concentrate on recently published titles rather than the classics from your childhood.) After reading several titles, identify which type of children's literature you enjoyed the most. This is probably the genre you would most enjoy writing in, too.

2. Read at least one article, poem, and book from each of the children's genres. After each reading selection, brainstorm three ideas that would be appropriate for that genre. Circle the one that appeals to you the most.

3. Join the Society of Children's Book Writers and Illustrators (SCBWI). For the price of postage you can receive updated book and magazine market guides. Send for them. When they arrive, study each publisher's entry. If you see something that catches your eye, send for the publisher's writers guidelines or a sample magazine to analyze.

---

and teachers who like them. They hurt when people tease them. They need parents to love them.

Books have never been more important. Reading develops children's imagination in ways that television and movies will never be able to do. That's why we must be familiar with today's children and what they are interested in. There's no better way to do that than by being around children.

Volunteer at a school or library. Help coach a team. If you are really brave, be a troop leader! Then, when you're with the kids, use a very important writing skill: listening. Listen to what kids say and how they say it. Find out what troubles the age group you want to write for. Take notes so you don't forget. It is true—children say the darndest things, so take notes of catchy phrases that you hear. When you go home and look at your notes, you may find a story staring you in the face.

A SELECTION OF CHILDREN'S LITERATURE

Title   Author

Picture Books

Song and Dance Man	Karen Ackerman
The Polar Express	Chris Van Allsburg
More Than Anything Else	Marie Bradby
The Important Book	Margaret Wise Brown
The Very Hungry Caterpillar	Eric Carle
Will Rogers: Larger Than Life	Debbie Dadey
Wilfrid Gordon McDonald Partridge	Mem Fox
The Cow Who Wouldn't Come Down	Paul Brett Johnson
Brown Bear, Brown Bear, What Do You See?	Bill Martin Jr.
How the Stars Fell Into the Sky: A Navajo Legend	Jerrie Oughton
The Big Orange Splot	Daniel M. Pinkwater
The Giving Tree	Shel Silverstein
Somebody Loves You, Mr. Hatch	Eileen Spinelli
Alexander and the Terrible, Horrible, No Good, Very Bad Day	Judith Viorst
Owl Moon	Jane Yolen

Easy Readers

Triplet Trouble series	Debbie Dadey and Marcia Jones
Spot books	Eric Hill
Frog and Toad books	Arnold Lobel
The Hundred Dresses	Eleanor Estes
Amelia Bedelia books	Peggy Parish
Junie B. Jones series	Barbara Park
Marvin Redpost series	Louis Sachar
The Cat in the Hat	Dr. Seuss
Nate the Great books	Marjorie Sharmat
The Velveteen Rabbit	Margery Williams

Chapter Books

Henry Huggins	Beverly Cleary
Frindle	Andrew Clements
Amber Brown series	Paula Danzinger
My Mom the Frog	Debbie Dadey
The Adventures of the Bailey School Kids and The Bailey City Monsters series	Debbie Dadey and Marcia Jones
Godzilla Ate My Homework	Marcia Jones
Ella Enchanted	Gail Carson Levine
The Magic Tree House series	Mary Pope Osborne
The Best School Year Ever	Barbara Robinson
Wayside School Is Falling Down	Louis Sachar
American Girls series	various authors
The Boxcar Children series	Gertrude Chandler Warner
Charlotte's Web	E.B. White

A SELECTION OF CHILDREN'S LITERATURE

Title	Author
Middle-Grade Novels	
On My Honor	Marion Dane Bauer
Tales of a Fourth Grade Nothing	Judy Blume
Prairie Songs	Pam Conrad
Walk Two Moons	Sharon Creech
The Whipping Boy	Sid Fleischman
Lily's Crossing	Patricia Reilly Giff
The View From Saturday	E.L. Konigsburg
A Wrinkle in Time	Madeleine L'Engle
Number the Stars	Lois Lowry
The Baby-Sitters Club series	Ann Martin
Shiloh	Phyllis Reynolds Naylor
Bridge to Terabithia	Katherine Paterson
Where the Red Fern Grows	Wilson Rawls
Harry Potter books	J.K. Rowling
Wringer	Jerry Spinelli
Goosebumps series	R.L. Stein
Young-Adult Novels	
The Face on the Milk Carton	Caroline B. Cooney
Sex Education	Jenny Davis
The Outsiders	S.E. Hinton
Gentlehands	M.E. Kerr
The Giver	Lois Lowry
Island of the Blue Dolphins	Scott O'Dell
Music From a Place Called Half Moon	Jerrie Oughton
Brian's Return	Gary Paulsen
Soldier's Heart	Gary Paulsen
Mine Eyes Have Seen	Ann Rinaldi
Missing May	Cynthia Rylant
Holes	Louis Sachar
The Pigman	Paul Zindel
Nonfiction	
Vacuum Cleaners	Elaine Marie Alphin
Trains	Byron Barton
If You Were Born a Kitten	Marion Dane Bauer
What Teens Need to Succeed: Proven, Practical Ways to Shape Your Own Future	Peter L. Benson, Pamela Espeland, and Judy Galbraith
While a Tree Was Growing	Jane Bosveld
Lincoln: A Photobiography	Russell Freedman
Sky Tree: Seeing Science Through Art	Thomas Locker
Vroom! Vroom! Making 'dozers, 'copters, trucks, and more	Judy Press
If You Made a Million	David M. Schwartz

Title	Author

Nonfiction (cont'd)

Math Curse	Jon Scieszka
Knots in My Yo-Yo String	Jerry Spinelli
Lewis Hayden and the War Against Slavery	Joel Strangis

Poetry

Ashley Bryan's ABC of African American Poetry	Ashley Bryan
Anna Banana: 101 Jump-Rope Rhymes	Joanna Cole
Tomie's Little Mother Goose	Tomie dePaola
Joyful Noise: Poems for Two Voices	Paul Fleischman
The Inner City Mother Goose	Eve Merriam
A Pizza the Size of the Sun	Jack Prelutsky
Imagine That!	Jack Prelutsky
Oh, the Places You'll Go!	Dr. Seuss
Lunch Money and Other Poems About School	Carol Diggory Shields
Where the Sidewalk Ends	Shel Silverstein
Twinkle, Twinkle Little Star	Iza Trapani
If I Were in Charge of the World and Other Worries	Judith Viorst

Magazines

Cobblestone
Cricket Magazine
Dolphin Log
Faces
Guideposts for Kids
Highlights for Children
Ranger Rick
Science World
Teen Magazine
Turtle Magazine for Preschool Kids
Zillions: Consumer Reports for Kids

What's Good

The world of children's publishing has grown and developed tremendously during the last fifty years. Although their needs are still the same, today's children are exposed to real-life issues by just turning on their televisions. Young readers today see wars, riots, and police car chases progress right before their eyes while they relax in the relative safety of their homes. This window to the raw world makes them much more knowledgeable and sophisticated. If readers have changed somewhat, that means writing intended for them must change, too.

TRY IT YOURSELF

1. Look for changing trends in children's literature by examining Caldecott- and Newbery-winning titles from each decade.
2. What is selling now? Check out a copy of *The Horn Book Magazine* or the *School Library Journal* for reviews of new children's books.
3. Spend several hours in a bookstore looking at newly released children's books.
4. What do you think makes good writing? Re-examine the books, articles, and poems you've been reading. Choose your favorite from each genre. Make a list of what you think makes the writing sparkle. Then, hang the list over your writing desk as a reminder of what you would like your writing to include.

Writing needs to "move" for today's children. Kids are used to seeing entire stories unfold during the time span of a cable movie. That means they're not likely to sit through pages and pages of description that interrupt the flow of a book's plot. A fresh, natural voice is needed to keep kids interested.

When writing for today's young readers, be ready to move your writing with action, dialogue, and vibrant language. That doesn't just go for fiction; it's true for nonfiction, too. A group of students once shared with us their criteria for good novels. Top on their lists was "sparkle words." Take a look at what else they suggested makes a good book.

WHAT MAKES A GOOD BOOK – WHAT KIDS SAY

Good books . . .
- ☆ Have sparkle words (unique and unusual vocabulary).
- ☆ Use dialogue.
- ☆ Include suspense so you feel like you're part of the story.
- ☆ Have humor when appropriate.
- ☆ Use similes and metaphors to make the writing visible.
- ☆ Are exciting and interesting.
- ☆ Are about problems and topics kids care about.
- ☆ Include likeable characters.
- ☆ Have a unique setting.
- ☆ Make you want to read more.

Summary

If you're starting to suspect you were crazy to think you could ever write a children's book, take this little test. Read several different types of children's books. Did you enjoy them? Did you hate them? If you didn't like the experience, chances are this book saved you several years of suffering. But if you enjoyed them and want to read more, then you are in the right place.

Writing for children can be rewarding, especially when an adoring child begs you for an autograph or when you receive a letter from a reader saying, "I never liked to read before. But then I read one of your books and now I love to read." Writing for children can be heartbreaking when your neighbor asks you if you'll "ever be good enough" to write for adults. Writing for children can be lonely. Most of the time it's just you and the computer.

To write for children you must love to write. You must *have* to write. Your day is not complete unless you've written. When you feel that way, then my friend, you are a writer.

So grab a pen and a journal. Turn on your computer and get ready to type. Let's get sparking!

THE BLANK PAGE

Great. You grabbed a pen, your journal is open, the computer is up and ready. You've been to the library, read current books, and you liked what you read. You know that, more than anything, you want to write for children.

But what happens now that your screen is blank, that little cursor is teasing you with its blinking-blinking-blinking, and you cry out, "I can't think of anything to write?" Or maybe you've spent three hours scribbling away. You stop to take a breath, glancing over the pages filled with words, and you moan, "These ideas are horrible."

What you need are ideas worthy of your valuable writing time. How do you find them?

At any given time loads of ideas are swirling and tumbling in our brains like clothes being tossed in a dryer. But have you ever noticed that when you sit down, turn on the computer, and press "tab" to start a new paragraph, all those ideas seem to disappear (just like the socks from your laundry)?

Part of the problem may be that the logical portion of your brain is dousing your creativity by focusing on being critical of your creative thinking.

The brain is divided into hemispheres, and each side is responsible for certain activities. The left side of the brain handles logical, linear tasks and processes the world by looking at parts of the whole. This logical hemisphere is responsible for step-by-step, systematic, sequential thinking like classifying, analyzing, ordering, assessing, making literal connections, and drawing cause-and-effect conclusions. All these things are involved in the all-important, rule-governed task of stringing together words to speak and write.

We like to envision the left hemisphere igniting like a string of firecrackers. You light one wick and the firecracker explodes, then another and then another, so you experience a pop-pop-pop series of explosions.

The right hemisphere of the brain isn't sequential. The right hemisphere thinks in random patterns. Rather than trying to make sense of the world by breaking it into recognizable parts, the right side of the brain looks at the whole and uses images instead of words. Since it doesn't rely on systematic methods, the right hemisphere is open to creative imaging, emotions, and metaphorical connections.

We think of the right hemisphere as a Fourth of July sparkler. Once ignited, a beautiful cluster of sparks crackle and pop, reaching out in random patterns.

LEFT BRAIN VS. RIGHT BRAIN

Left Brain	Right Brain
Logical	Creative
Linear	Random
Literal	Metaphorical
Critic	Muse

Effective writing requires cooperation between both hemispheres. Unfortunately, when the right hemisphere sparkles with images and random explosions of thought, the critical left brain often kicks into gear saying things like, "What are you thinking? You can't write that! This isn't appropriate! You can't begin until you have a killer first line. Your teachers would never approve. Your parents will be devastated!"

Writers often let the systematic left hemisphere suppress the random images from the right hemisphere. In other words, part of your brain is critical and another part of your brain is inspirational. We think of the hemispheres as our critic and our muse.

The good news is that the strategies in this chapter help writers encourage both sides of the brain—the creative muse and the logical critic—to work in cooperation to generate unique and exciting ideas. Here's a list of the topics we'll tackle:

Brainstorming
Webbing
Freewriting
Listing
Questioning
Researching
The Five Senses
Overheard Conversations
Dialogues
Letters (Real and Fictional)
The Big Idea
What-iffing
Thinking Small
Pictures
Pet Peeves
Reading
Forced Relationships
Time Lines
Possessions
Doodling
In My Shoes
Musical Muse

Brainstorming

Brainstorming . . . the word alone conjures powerful images. It should—brainstorming is a powerful tool for generating ideas and later developing those ideas. The rest of this chapter will introduce specific idea-generating strategies. Each strategy relies on the basic theory behind brainstorming.

Brainstorming is often thought of as a group problem-solving activity during which each member of the group contributes ideas. The rules are simple. Anything goes; no judgments are allowed; all ideas are recorded. Piggybacking, or spinning off of others' ideas, is allowed and encouraged.

Brainstorming is like using the Internet. You start your search with one idea, finding a site that lists a related link. You click on that link and you discover a new site with even more links. The more you click, the more the world of possibilities opens up to you.

TRY IT YOURSELF: BRAINSTORMING

Brainstorm the following.

1. Possessions
2. Courage
3. The worst day ever
4. Spaceships
5. Oops
6. Animal heroes
7. Hiding in the closet
8. Grandpa's story
9. The silver dollar
10. Intriguing characters

At a recent monthly meeting of Marcia's critique group (more about critique groups in chapter 8) Paul Brett Johnson asked for help generating ideas for a new picture book. "I need help with the ending," he told the group. He had a great cast of animal characters and a terrific conflict centered around a package found at the post office without a delivery address the week before Christmas. But he had not been able to come up with a strong ending. That's when the brainstorming began.

"Maybe the box was empty."

"What if an animal chewed through the paper?"

"How about if the town members sneaked in and peeked at what was inside?"

"What would happen if someone stole what was in the package?"

As a group, we called out possible ideas as Paul furiously scribbled them all down. Some of the ideas were pretty wild, some were clichés, some were downright stupid. It didn't matter because those ideas led to other ideas.

"We've reached a dead end," one writer said. It seemed as though she was right. We all sat there. Silent.

Suddenly, another writer, Becky North, sat up straight. "I've got it," she said. And she did. She had the perfect idea for Paul's ending.

At the end of twenty minutes, Paul had at least three strong ideas for the ending, one of which he was able to use.

People are often frustrated when they reach a lull in a brainstorming session. But Becky did what good creative thinkers must do. She kept her mind open. The truth is, the first ideas during brainstorming are usually not the best—that's why they pop into your head so easily. The best ideas are the ones you have to work for.

Even though brainstorming was first thought of as a group activity, it can help writers who are working alone. That's because each of us always has a group of two with whom to brainstorm—the parts of our brains that act as the critic and the muse.

Now that you know about brainstorming, try sparking your creativity by brainstorming some of the ideas on page 32. Try it with a group of other writers, or just sit down and brainstorm with your personal critic and muse participating. Remember: Write down all your ideas, and no censoring allowed!

Webbing

Webbing is an activity that goes by many names, including ballooning, clustering, and mind mapping. No matter what you call it, it is one of the most effective ways to ignite idea sparks.

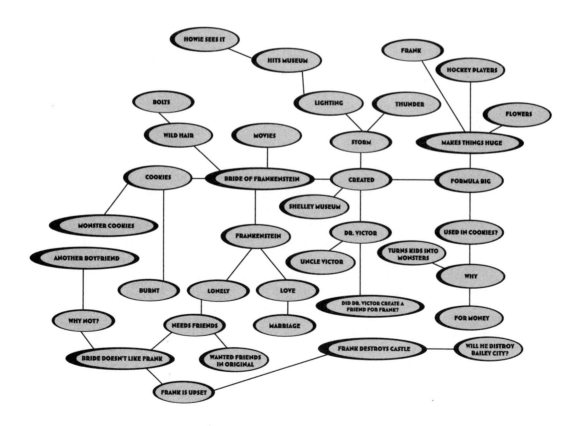

TRY IT YOURSELF: WEBBING

Web the following.

1. Fear
2. Friendship
3. Pets
4. Embarrassment
5. Sky
6. Teachers
7. Lessons learned
8. Hate
9. Spring
10. Competition

Webbing lets you splatter ideas in a free, nonlinear format so your creative muse is happy, but it also keeps track of connections in a linear fashion so your critic doesn't stress out. Webbing is useful when you're staring at the blank page. It's also helpful as you try to organize ideas for chapters of longer pieces.

Webbing is done by all ages; even kindergartners. That's how easy it is! This is all you need to remember. Start with an idea, word, or phrase and put it in the center of your paper. Put a circle around it as a hint to your brain to remember the "central" idea. Then, free-associate! Jot down on the paper whatever your brain blurts out. Circle the brainstormed ideas and draw lines from the central idea to the ideas you brainstorm. This reminds your creative muse that all these ideas are connected and also satisfies your critic by showing the linear flow of ideas. Keep going until you sense a shift from random association to a more focused cluster around a subtopic. The end result looks something like dandelion seeds ready to be scattered by the wind.

Examine your web. Are there ideas demanding to be connected to other ideas? Are there dense areas of lines and circles where many ideas are clustered? Take a look at an example of webbing from our book *Bride of Frankenstein Doesn't Bake Cookies* on page 33.

Notice how many ideas connect to the words "created" and "Frankenstein." We decided to concentrate on these ideas, although we used many of the other ideas, too. This is the way a web works. It is not only a way to develop ideas, but also a method to focus those ideas in a particular direction.

Now that you know about webbing, try some webbing sparks of your own. Put one of the topics on page 34 in the center of the paper, then start free-associating. Remember . . . anything goes!

Freewriting

Writing. There is so much to think about—capitals; periods; when to start a new paragraph; spelling; typing errors; creating believable characters; plotting with suspense; chapter hooks; writing with authority; worrying about if the idea is good; wondering if your writing sparkles. Just think about it!

On second thought, *don't think about it*! In fact, thinking is often what keeps writers from writing. Worrying about writing will only send your muse into hiding. After all, why should your muse risk being creative when there are so many things that can go wrong?

Instead of worrying, the best thing to do is to stop thinking and just write. Flow write—typing or writing as fast as you can without stopping for five or ten minutes. Write free, unfettered by worries of technique, style, or content. Just write.

Freewriting allows your muse to speak without risk. In her book *Wild Minds*, Natalie Goldberg states that she used freewriting to help her "learn to cut through first thoughts," and that freewriting helps writers "learn about cutting through resistance."

There are few guidelines, rules, or risks when you freewrite. To freewrite, all you need is a few minutes of your time.

TRY IT YOURSELF: FREEWRITING

Spark your writing by freewriting about the following. Remember: Write fast, don't stop, and no worrying allowed!

1. Getting into trouble . . .
2. Talking back . . .
3. One time I felt really proud . . .
4. What I really want . . .
5. Secrets . . .
6. My earliest memory . . .
7. If I was brave enough . . .
8. What I really believe . . .
9. My biggest loss . . .
10. My hardest sacrifice . . .

Open your journal or sit down at the computer, and start writing. Don't stop. That's the real trick. Stopping only gives your critic time to butt in with those pesky warnings. Forcing words on the paper keeps the critic at bay and gives your muse a chance to flow through your fingers. So don't stop. If you run out of things to say, list items on your desk, list favorite foods, all the things that bother you, or write about how you don't have anything to write about. Soon, your muse will get motivated again and off you'll go. Freewriting gives you permission— the freedom—to write pages and pages of junk because your critic knows that this isn't "for real." It also lets you get rid of all those bits and pieces of everyday life that might be getting in the way of your muse.

"Junk!" we heard you yell. "We don't want to write junk!"

Don't worry. The more you write the more likely you'll discover bright sparks buried in all that muddy writing. Start with just a few minutes, maybe five. You'll soon find out those five minutes have grown to ten or fifteen.

Freewriting is great for journaling, breaking the evil spell of the blank page, or for getting started on the next section of a longer piece. "How?" you ask. Try this. Pretend you're writing an intermediate chapter book set during the Civil War. The protagonist is hiding in the woods of Virginia when a dog discovers him. What happens? Open your journal and start writing. Don't stop. Just write for a full ten minutes.

TRY IT YOURSELF: LISTING

Practice sparking your thinking by using lists. Make lists of fifty—or even better, one hundred thoughts—about the following. Remember to write fast and don't worry about repeating. Once you've finished a list, look for clusters of ideas that might work for a writing piece.

1. Accomplishments
2. Things to try
3. Adventurous places
4. Character traits
5. Problems kids face
6. Brave things kids do
7. What kids care about
8. What adults care about
9. Interesting topics
10. Things worth praying for

Listing

We all know what a list is. We make lists reminding us what to get at the grocery store, what errands we need to write, to whom we need to send holiday greetings, what presents we hope to receive for our next big birthday. But have you thought about listing to help you generate ideas or to get started on that best-seller you want to write?

Listing is one of the easiest strategies to use. All you need to do is think of a topic and then jot down what comes to mind. But unlike a grocery list, make sure your critic doesn't interfere with playful thought. It's important to make your list fast, free, and fun. Don't worry if you find yourself repeating words, ideas, and phrases. Just keep listing. Try for a list of fifty. Better yet, go for one hundred.

Let's say you're sitting at your desk, staring at a beautiful white and totally clean piece of paper. You need an idea to help you get started on a new article for a children's magazine story. You know you want to write about ants, but what will be the focus? Start by making a list. Here is our list as an example.

FREE FORM LIST

Ants

1. Types of ants
2. Ants in the winter
3. Do ants get blown away in the wind?
4. Do ants drown when it rains?
5. Why ants march in lines
6. How ants carry such big crumbs of bread
7. Favorite foods of ants
8. Foods ants won't touch
9. Ant-free picnics
10. Strength of ants compared to humans
11. Tunneling systems of ants
12. Social structure
13. Job divisions
14. Why ants are different colors
15. How ants build mounds that look like Egyptian pyramids
16. Biting ants
17. Harmless ants
18. Fire ants
19. Treatment of ant bites
20. Body of ants
21. Ant farming
22. Lessons to learn from ants
23. Cooperation
24. Job specialization
25. How ants use their antennae
26. Ants in the house
27. How to avoid ant bites
28. Ants as architects
29. How do they know how to build an ant hill?
30. How do they work together to dig their tunnels?
31. Can ants build tunnels in all kinds of soil?
32. The best and worst dirt for ants
33. Where to find ants
34. Do ants live in their tunnels forever or do they move?
35. Why do ants always look so busy?
36. Are ants poisonous?
37. What are the functions of the three body parts?
38. How fast can an ant move?
39. Are some ants faster than others?
40. What are the biggest and smallest ants?
41. How long does it take to build an anthill?
42. Do ants ever get in trouble for being lazy?
43. Do ants sleep?
44. Do ants trip on their six legs?
45. Fighting ants
46. Ant diseases
47. Importance of ants
48. Treating ant bites
49. Ants in your pants—where did the saying originate?
50. How many ants live in my yard?

"Hey!" you just yelled. "You repeated ideas."

Yep, you're right. Repeating is fine. In fact, looking at the patterns of thought can help you organize your thoughts for writing.

Once a list has been produced, look for patterns of repeated ideas and concepts. Using different-colored highlighting pens can help. In looking at the example, there are definite categories of ideas including ant tunnels/hills, ant bites, and the bodies of ants. Once the categories have been determined, you can organize your list into clusters for possible writing. Take a look at the following chart to see what we mean.

ORGANIZED LIST

Ants

Ant Behavior	Ant Physiology	Ant Bites	Ant Architects
Marching	Relative strength	Biting ants	Tunneling systems
Carrying big loads	Colors	Harmless ants	Job divisions and
Eating	Bodies	Fire ants	specialization
Social structure	Antennae	Bite treatment	Ant mounds/hills
Job divisions/ Job	Body part functions	Avoiding bites	How long it takes to
specialization	Sizes	Poisonous ants	build tunnels/hills
Perseverance	Legs	Ants in your pants	Cooperation during
Cooperation	Diseases		construction
Motivation			Soil and tunnels
			Finding tunnels
			How long a tunnel lasts
			How tunnels and hills
			survive rain and wind

Questioning

"Why is the grass green?" "Why can't girls pee standing up?" "How did God make the sky?"

Kids are pros at asking questions. So good, in fact, that many of us cringe when we feel that all-too-familiar tug on our shirtsleeves. But we shouldn't dread those questions. We need to listen to them. Questioning is a great way to jerk your brain on to a new path of thinking. It's also a wonderful strategy for producing writing ideas.

Like listing, the goal is to write fast. You can list questions about a specific writing topic, or if you're really stumped for a writing idea, just start listing questions that kids might ask. Here are a few examples.

1. How does grass grow?
2. Do teachers go to the bathroom?

TRY IT YOURSELF: QUESTIONING

List as many questions as you can about the following.
1. Wombats
2. Friendship
3. Stealth fighters
4. Scabs
5. Parents
6. Secrets
7. Soccer
8. Fighting
9. Friends
10. Inventions

---

3. Why are most roofs black?
4. How do postal workers plan their routes?
5. Why are stop signs red and yield signs yellow?
6. Who makes computer games?
7. How does a fax machine work?
8. Is it OK to stomp on bugs?
9. What do you do if you find a bat clinging to the basement wall?
10. Do worms sleep?
11. What makes wind?
12. Why do people plant daffodils but pull up dandelions when they're both yellow flowers?
13. How is toilet paper made?
14. Why do kids have to do homework?
15. How many snowflakes does it take to make a snowball?

Researching

The library is a treasure trove of ideas. If you don't believe us, stop by your closest library and start browsing. Take a notepad to jot down interesting ideas you discover while perusing the shelves. If you have the time, volunteer at a school or public library and help shelve books. Ideas will overwhelm you as you allow yourself to see all the many types of books. Debbie came up with the idea for writing *Shooting Star: Annie Oakley, the Legend* after shelving tall tale after tall tale about male heroes. It seemed only fair that girls should have tall-tale heroes, too.

TRY IT YOURSELF: RESEARCHING

1. Find out about kids and life in a covered wagon.
2. Find out about the desert. What would it be like to live there?
3. Child labor is a reality in many countries, even today. What is it like?
4. What if a young girl didn't want to get married or become a nun in the Middle Ages?
5. Pages helped knights. Did the pages accompany the knights on travels far from home and in battles?
6. What was it like to be a child of a mobster living in Chicago in 1920?
7. Your father works for a lumbering company that cuts trees. What is that like (especially since you are very ecologically minded)?
8. What was it like for a young child to live in a coal mining town in the 1920s?
9. What was it like to be a Native American on the Trail of Tears?
10. What was it like to be a young calvary soldier chasing Chief Joseph?

The library is also the place to dig for ideas. Since many of our books are about folkloric creatures, we use the library to learn about new creatures and to find details that enhance our stories. Invariably we find something that leads us toward a new story idea. Newbery Award–winner Russell Freedman refuses to let anyone do his research for him because he believes in serendipity. There is always that fascinating fact that he comes across while doing research that leads him to explore new ideas for his existing story idea, or perhaps for another. Without library research, the facts would still lie buried, and so would the ideas.

Is there something that has always fascinated you, but somehow you never researched it? Now is the time. Go to the library and discover.

The Five Senses

Close your eyes. Breathe deep. Can you smell them? Grandma's sugar cookies. Crisp around the edges, but so soft in the center they nearly melt when you bite into them. They're covered with sour-cream icing sprinkled with colorful candies. She baked them just for visitors and

TRY IT YOURSELF: THE FIVE SENSES

Try the following exercises to encourage your senses to trigger memories worth writing about.

1. Go outside and sit in a lawn chair with your eyes closed. Pay attention to what you hear.
2. Open your spice cabinet. Try sniffing jars of chili powder, cinnamon, and cloves.
3. Go to a park and sit on a bench. What do you *really* see?
4. Walk through a department store and let your fingers play through the racks of clothes. What do the textures remind you of?
5. (Warning: This is the best exercise in the entire book! We expect everyone to try it several times!) Go to a local ice-cream shop and treat yourself to your favorite ice-cream dessert. It's even better if there is a mixture of tastes (like in a hot fudge sundae or a banana split)! Eat it slowly. What childhood memories come to mind?

---

kept them in the black cookie jar with fruit painted on the side.

Or maybe your window is open and a spring breeze billows the sheers, causing you to shiver. It reminds you of that night on the beach when you were ten. It was early evening and you put on a sweatshirt because the breeze ruffling the ocean was sending shivers down your arms. It was too cold for bathing suits so your dad bought a Frisbee and tossed it to you over and over. No matter how hard you tried, the ocean breeze caught the disk and sent it twirling in a crazy arch so it landed far from your Dad. Both of you laughed so hard your sides hurt.

Our five senses can be an exciting starting point for story ideas. Because our senses bring back such strong memories, they trigger ideas that have long laid dormant in the backs of our minds. Pay attention to your five senses as you write. Could one be a springboard to a great writing piece?

1. What does Christmas smell like?
2. What are the sounds of a playground?
3. What did your first horseback ride smell like?
4. What are the sounds of an ice-cream shop?
5. What did it sound like at the beach on a windy day?
6. What did the school cafeteria really smell like?
7. What were the sounds in the classroom when your teacher said,

"Put your heads down"?

8. What did Santa really look like when you were four years old?
9. How do your dog's ears really feel?
10. How did it feel when your mother stroked your hair?

Our five senses provide a strong connection to our memories, so don't hesitate to take advantage of them.

Overheard Conversations

One of the best ways to get ideas is to be sneaky. Sit on a playground or in a crowded restaurant frequented by kids and open your ears. What are those kids and parents talking about? Try to take notes without being noticed. The longer you sit the more you'll hear and the less obvious you'll be.

Sometimes the conversations may be enough to start a story all by itself. For instance, say you heard a thirteen-year-old girl dressed in dirty jeans say, "I'm not going to invite Kim to my party! She's mean!" Immediately, you wonder if you should feel sorry for Kim or for the party person. Maybe Kim really is mean and will ruin the party for everyone.

TRY IT YOURSELF: OVERHEARD CONVERSATIONS

Use the following suggestions to get started using overheard conversations.

1. Volunteer at a school or public library. While you're putting books away, listen to the patrons chat. Write down anything that catches your fancy.
2. Visit a local fast-food chain at dinnertime. Listen to the parents fuss at the kids and let your mind wander. What happens when the kids get home? Do they get a story before going to bed, or do they fall asleep on the floor whenever they feel like it?
3. Read the dialogue aloud from a children's book that you don't know. Select a passage at random, and design your own story idea around it.
4. Talk to a teacher at a local school. Ask her to tell you about her worst teaching day. (If the conversation sparks an idea, be sure to dedicate the book to that teacher!)
5. Talk to kids about what they hate about school. What would they do to change things?

Here's another example. You're in a mall and you hear an eight-year-old boy complain, "My dad lied to me." What did he lie about? Did he promise a pony? Did he promise to come to the school open house? Did he promise to never drink again?

You can ask so many questions from one little snippet of conversation, and each question can spark a story idea. All we have to do is clean out our ears, dust off our sleuthing skills, and listen.

Dialogues

Fictional dialogues are also great at helping you get unstuck. Fictional dialogues are written like real conversations, only they never really happen.

Fictional dialogues are conversations between characters or props. This natural flow of conversation can help you get to the heart of your story, article, or poem.

TRY IT YOURSELF: DIALOGUES

1. Write dialogues for the following.
   * an argument between two characters
   * an introduction between the tree house and the tree
   * a meeting between a squirrel and a hawk living in the forest
   * a conversation between the neighbor who sees kids carting off wood and one of the children's parents
   * a warning from the tree standing guard where the path begins to the dog that follows his owner into the darkness of the forest

2. Here's another example. You're thinking about writing an article on the postal service and you can't think of how to start. Try writing dialogues between the mailbox and the:
   * dogs in the neighborhood
   * letters waiting to be mailed
   * postal carrier who slams the mailbox door too hard

3. Or perhaps your poem about prejudice is muddled by ambiguous introspection. Find a clearer focus by writing dialogues between characters who are:
   * skinny and fat
   * African American and Asian
   * young and old
   * poor and rich
   * Hispanic and white

For instance, in Maurice Sendak's *Where the Wild Things Are*, Max could have had an argument with his mother.

"Take that silly costume off and behave," Max's mother yelled.

Max jumped onto the table and screamed. "I am not Max. I'm a wild thing and I'll do whatever I want!"

The previous fictional dialogue did not actually happen, but it certainly could have set the mood for the rest of the story. Now it's time to try your hand at it with the "Try It Yourself" exercises on page 43.

Letters

Why is it we never worry about "speaker's block" before blurting out what we're thinking, but we've all experienced the fear of putting those same words on paper? Have you noticed that as you talk, more ideas spew forth, unbidden? Sometimes, at least for us, those spoken ideas come *too* easily! Well, the same can be true for our written words. We just need to give our writing the same freedom we allow our spoken words.

Writing is spoken language put on paper. It's made of the same stuff we use to tell our best friend about the fight we had, our mothers about our worries, our husbands about our day, or our children about what it was like when we were growing up. It's all made from words.

Capture some of the same spontaneity of the spoken word by writing letters. Instead of worrying over plot and character, let your ideas flow as if you're having a friendly conversation. Sit down and write a letter. (Don't worry, you don't have to send it unless you really want to!) After all, your stories, articles, and poems are communication between you and your readers—think of them like letters between you and your audience.

Letter writing helps your writing in other ways, too. It promotes development of a natural writer's voice and keeps you focused on the intended audience. Somewhere deep in your letter, an idea may appear—one that has been buried deep inside. Letter writing can bring that forgotten thought or idea to the surface, where it can be nurtured, toyed with, mulled over, and eventually developed into a story.

There are two types of letter writing: real letters and fictional letters. Both are valuable idea-generating tools for writers.

Real Letters

Do you remember the excitement of going to the mailbox and finding something other than bills and advertisements? Rekindle that excitement by writing letters to your family and friends. Fill your letter with

TRY IT YOURSELF: LETTERS

Write letters from:

1. Your story's "hero" to the "villain"
2. You to a reader explaining what you hope she will gain from reading your story, article, or poem
3. Your story's antagonist to you
4. Your muse to yourself
5. Your present self to your future self
6. Yourself as a child to your present self
7. Your present self to the kid that hurt your feelings in the fifth grade
8. Your fourth-grade self to the teacher who humiliated you in front of the class
9. Your computer to yourself about the touch of your fingers on the keyboard
10. Your childhood bicycle to you

---

the details of your life, ponderings of the past, and hopes for the future. Make a copy for yourself, slap a stamp on it, and send it off.

The neat thing about letter writing is that you stay in contact with friends and family. They will marvel at your witty and thoughtful letters, while all the time you are writing those letters you are actually working on story ideas. Don't you just love two-for-one specials?

After writing your letter, look closely at what you've written. Our lives are filled with story fodder. Look at Marcia's example on page 46 and see if you can find story ideas.

Did you see any story sparks in the sample letter? Here are a few we came up with.

1. Sisters who are always in trouble
2. Separation of family members
3. Uncontrollable giggles that get a kid in trouble
4. Kids trying to hide a broken valuable
5. A magazine article on suction

The great thing about real letters you send is that you can anticipate receiving answers. Analyze those letters for story sparks the same way you search the letters you write.

Dear Sis,

I was pushing my cart during my weekly trip to the grocery the other day when a tiny toilet plunger caught my eye. The next thing I knew I was giggling so hard a passing shopper looked at me like I should be wearing a funny white jacket. But I couldn't help it because the sight of that plunger reminded me of that time you and I found a little plunger in the linen closet.

It wasn't like most plungers. This one was only about a foot high. We didn't know how powerful that cute little plunger could be! Remember how we plopped it down on the floor to try it out? That plunger latched onto the black-and-white bathroom linoleum so hard it was like it had taken root for life. We pulled and tugged until finally it came loose with a giant ripping sound. We got the plunger up all right, along with half of a linoleum square. We tried gluing the linoleum back down, but it didn't work. We thought we would be grounded for life! Getting in trouble with you was so much fun!

I wish you and I could have some of those fun times again. But I won't allow old age to dim those fun memories!

Love always,

Marcia

P.S. I bought the little plunger!

Fictional Letters

Take a deep breath and stop worrying. You don't have to really send the letters you write. In fact, some letters should not be sent, but they are still useful tools for finding writing ideas.

Fictional letters encourage a natural writing voice while helping you focus on the purpose of your piece even more than real letters do. Since you know these letters will never be sent, your critic won't mind stepping aside and letting your writing really rip.

You can use an unsent letter to dig for story sparks or to clarify a scene. Try it and see. You might be surprised what develops as you write letters never meant to be sent. Use the "Try It Yourself" exercises on page 45 to get you started.

The Big Idea

Hey! What's the big idea?

Everybody has beliefs; what are yours? What do you believe to be true about life? Analyzing your own beliefs can become a rich source of story material. But be warned, this exercise requires honest introspection!

Identifying what you believe to be true about the big picture of life is a simple process. Just ask yourself one question about big ideas: What do you believe? Then be ready to write down your raw feelings and opinions. Once the list is done, relate a big idea to a kid situation.

When Marcia was digging for an idea for one of her books, she used this exercise to find a story focus. Here is the question and the responses she jotted down.

"What do I believe to be true about *differences*?"

* ★ Differences can be good.
* ★ Differences can result in prejudice.
* ★ Differences may result in conflict.
* ★ Wars are caused by differences.
* ★ Differences can be seen and not seen.
* ★ There are differences of opinion and beliefs.
* ★ There are physical differences.
* ★ Change and growth result in becoming different.
* ★ Indifferent means you just don't care, so does different mean you care?

TRY IT YOURSELF: THE BIG IDEA

What do you believe to be true about the following big ideas?

1. Honor
2. Fear
3. Relationships
4. Changes
5. Betrayal
6. Power
7. Secrets
8. Differences
9. Competition
10. Loss

★ It takes courage to be different.

★ It takes an open mind to accept differences.

★ Differences may be difficult to understand.

★ Everybody is different.

★ Some people thrive on being different.

★ Some people like being the same as everybody else.

★ Peer pressure preys on differences.

Did anything from her list spark your interest?

Marcia liked the idea that it takes courage to be different. She developed a story about a Kansas prairie girl in the 1800s who finds the courage to think differently than her family and friends about African Americans fleeing the war-torn South.

So, what's your big idea? Find out by trying some of the exercises on page 47. Once you've listed your beliefs, look over your lists and think of at least three kid situations related to your big ideas.

What If?

One of the easiest roads to finding new ideas is to take a normal situation and say, "What if?" What-ifs can be as wild as your imagination will let you roam. In our first book, *Vampires Don't Wear Polka Dots*, we

TRY IT YOURSELF: WHAT IF?

1. What if the postman brought you a letter from an aunt you didn't even know you had?
2. What if your underwear drawer started talking to you?
3. What if your house reminded you to do your chores, just like some cars remind you to put on your seat belts?
4. What if you couldn't walk anymore?
5. What if your school was on the other side of a big river and there was no bridge?
6. What if your brother stole something very important to you and wouldn't give it back?
7. What if everyone else in your class could run faster than you?
8. What if you woke up one morning with green teeth?
9. What if you would only eat strawberries?
10. What if your teacher embarrassed someone every day and today was your day?

took the ordinary situation of a third-grade class and said, "What if the third-grade teacher really was a vampire?" We kept what-iffing until we had the beginnings of a story.

"What if a group of kids are so bad they chase off their teacher?"

"What if they suspect their new teacher really is a vampire?"

"What if the new teacher moves into a haunted house?"

"What if the kids suspect their teacher has magic power?"

"What if one of the kids pushes the new teacher too far?"

What-iffing is incredibly easy and fun. It's also one of the most powerful strategies available to writers.

Look at a home or school situation and give it a slight twist. Put two things that normally wouldn't go together and see what happens. Let your mind wander in new directions. The best possibilities are ones that you find most interesting, but you might like to try some of the suggestions on page 48 to get started what-iffing.

Thinking Small

The enormity of writing is often overwhelming. Sometimes, we're blind to our ideas because we're too busy stressing over the complete project. One way to help regain your vision is to think small.

Anne Lamott recommends using short assignments. She keeps a

TRY IT YOURSELF: THINKING SMALL

1. If you're really brave, try this exercise in public. Take your one-inch frame to the following places and write what you see.

☆ The mall   ☆ Your backyard

☆ A grocery store   ☆ In a classroom

☆ A playground   ☆ In your child's bedroom

☆ A church   ☆ At the local animal shelter

☆ A soccer game   ☆ At the airport

2. Hold up your one-inch frame. Look through it and write what you imagine about:

☆ A character's expression

☆ The setting of your novel

☆ A description of your article's topic

☆ A central metaphor for your poem

☆ One dialogue exchange between your antagonist and protagonist.

one-inch picture frame on her desk to remind her that she only has "to pick up the one-inch picture frame to figure out a one-inch piece of my story to tell, one small scene, one memory, one exchange."

Try it. Make a one-inch frame from cardboard. Hold it up. Don't worry about your novel. Push the thought of your article out of your mind. What do you see through the frame?

Your one-inch picture frame is a handy tool for jump-starting your writing when you're in the middle of a project, too. The task of completing a piece is daunting. Instead of worrying about the entire book, article, or poem, use your one-inch frame to concentrate your energy on just a small part. Experiment with some of the exercises on page 49.

TRY IT YOURSELF: PICTURES

Here are some suggestions to help you get started with thinking in pictures.

1. Open up a magazine and point to a picture at random. Jot down a paragraph about the people in the picture. What are they doing? What are they thinking?

2. Look at a children's book and pick one illustration. Find one character who is not the main character. Let your mind wander and make up a life for this character apart from the book.

3. Find old family photographs. Perhaps they are of family members you don't even know. Now is your chance to get to know them on your own terms. Maybe they had a secret life that their whole family was involved in, like making moonshine.

4. Find an interesting picture in an old annual. Give that person a birthday, a new name, hobbies, and friends. In other words, create a life for her and in turn create the nucleus of a story: the main character.

5. Find a picture book with interesting pictures that you've never read before. Cover up the text and write your own story. It's OK if you start departing from the existing pictures. In fact, that's the plan. But the original pictures got you started and that's what we sometimes need—a little boost in the right direction.

6. Get out a picture of yourself when you were eight years old. What were you like then? Can you remember the day that picture was taken? Write a paragraph about that day.

Pictures

Speaking of picture frames, what about what's inside some of your old frames? Laurie Lawlor loves to look at old photos to get ideas. She stares at the photos and tries to imagine what the people in the photo's life must have been like. Were they smiling for the photo? Were they unhappy? How did that stain get on their clothes? Did they get in trouble for the stain? What happened to them the day after the photo?

Let your mind go wild with all sorts of questions, and since the answers are usually unknown, you can answer them however you want. You can make up names and situations. Having the photo in front of you while you write will give you a focal point and help you describe your characters. Look closely at the photo. You might even want to get out a magnifying glass to find details you might otherwise miss.

Sometimes, you might want to research to see if you can find out truths about the real people in the picture. Your research could involve talking to relatives or friends. You can always embellish the truth and fictionalize it if you're planning on writing a novel. Or perhaps you will want to research at the library about the time in which the photo was taken. This will give your idea legs and help you develop your story. Try it yourself with the exercises on page 50.

Pet Peeves

Let's face it: If everything was hunky-dory all the time, most stories would be pretty boring. As in all works of fiction, children's books have conflicts. Something is wrong and the problem gets worse before the story is resolved. A story may have more than one conflict, although one should be most dominant.

If we look within ourselves, we realize that the things that irritate us most are the things we feel strongly about. Those conflicts are what we can write about with great emotion, and that can turn into our best writing. Think for a moment about the things that bother you most now. Make a list. Perhaps your list is full of simple pet peeves or full-blown conflicts.

Turn the clock back twenty years. What bothered you then? Make a list of ten things. Now, turn the clock back thirty years (of course this depends on your age). What bothered you then? Was it the big girl on the bus who always pulled your hair and made fun of you? Make a list of ten things that bothered you. Pick two of the ones you felt most strongly about. Write a paragraph about those two conflicts. Now, can you put those two conflicts together in a story idea? Try it in one paragraph and see what happens. If you like the result, you have the gold that creates a story.

TRY IT YOURSELF: PET PEEVES

Try the following activity to create more conflict in your writing life.

1. Select a Newbery-winning book from the list in chapter 1. Read it and determine what type of conflict or conflicts were in the book. Can you think of similar conflicts in your life or in friends' lives? Jot them down to create your own conflict list.

2. Find a Caldecott-winning book to read from the list in chapter 1. Is there a conflict? It might be tougher to find in a picture book, but it will probably still be there. Can you think of a similar conflict to add to your conflict list?

3. This is a tough exercise, but give it a try. Make up three different ideas to fit these conflicts: Man against nature; man against man; man against himself. There may be a nugget of an idea inside those conflicts.

4. Parental conflicts are perhaps the most heartrending for a child. Pretend you are a child listening to parents fight. What are you feeling?

5. A lot of books are written about bullies, but rarely from the bully's viewpoint. Pretend you are the bully. What are you feeling when you see the playground?

Reading

We all love reading; writers have to. Some of us love reading so much it actually interferes with our writing. Instead of feeling guilty, try using your reading to your advantage. Marcia allows herself to read, but she challenges herself to develop at least three ideas for every book she reads. Once, she read a book in which a character had trouble keeping friends. The character happened to have a guinea pig. After reading the book, she came up with these three ideas:

1. The guinea pig that ate New York—including all the homework.
2. The worst best friend in the world—about a kid who keeps making mistakes that jeopardize his friendship.
3. Winner's Circle—to get in the club you have to be a winner, but Madison has never won anything in her life. How can she get in the club?

After studying her list she wrote *Godzilla Ate My Homework*, a story about a second grader named Parker who ends up in big trouble when his pet guinea pig named Godzilla starts eating everything in sight.

So, go ahead—read. But, don't neglect your writing.

TRY IT YOURSELF: READING

Take Marcia's challenge! Try the following reading activities to develop ideas for your next best-seller.

1. Read a chapter book and "what-if" three ideas about a similar character.
2. Read a fairy tale, then list three ideas for a modern-day fairy tale.
3. Read a nonfiction book or article and write three questions for follow-up articles or books.
4. Use the first line of an existing book to start your own story. When you've finished your story, go back and change that first line.

Forced Relationships

Here's a surefire way to spark a lazy muse: Force a relationship between two unlike items or ideas. This is a playful way to nudge your muse into creative thought. It's also great for developing clever metaphors while writing. Not sure what we have in mind? Try this: Open up the dictionary and point to a word. Do it again. Now, tell how the two unrelated concepts are alike. Did the exercise ignite a spark for a story?

Try something else. Pretend you're writing a story about a kid who is going to a new school. Spark your writing by forcing an analogous relationship. Compare the first day at a new school to a hurricane. Begin by listing attributes of a hurricane. Your list might look like the following:

Rain
Wind
Eye of the storm
Debris
Circular
Classes of storms
Names
Clouds
Calm of the eye
Low/high tides
Boarded windows
Straws driven through trees
Flooding

TRY IT YOURSELF: FORCED RELATIONSHIPS

1. It's your turn. Try some of the following analogous relationships to link two things you might not normally connect.
   - ✷ How is the weekend like a spider's web?
   - ✷ How is friendship like a baseball game?
   - ✷ How is homework like a rainbow?
   - ✷ How is a swing set like having a fight?
   - ✷ How is competition like a rose?

2. Select one item from your home. Then go to the grocery store and pick out an item. Somehow create a story idea from those two items. Debbie's was "Cowboy boots and the Broccoli Bunch." Now she has to develop that idea into a fascinating story.

3. Get a mail-order catalog and close your eyes. Flip through the pages and point. Open your eyes and see where you've landed. Do the same thing again with a different catalog. Can you create a story idea from the two items? When Debbie did it she came up with jeans and bubbles.

4. Pick something from your refrigerator and pair it with underwear. (Underwear is always good for a laugh with kids.) Let your mind wander and see what story idea these two unrelated items can create.

Now that you have a list, use those attributes to describe the first day of school. Here's our example.

Kayla's first day of school started out like the calm before a storm. Then her alarm went off, and she felt the first clouds roll in. She wanted to wear jeans and a T-shirt, but her Mom said the first day of school called for special clothes. Hurricane Kayla hit full blast when she looked around her new classroom. Of course, she was the only girl in a dress. Everybody else wore jeans, shorts, and T-shirts. A girl in the front row laughed, and it felt like hailstones striking as Kayla walked to the last desk in the third row. By the end of her first day at school, Kayla had her windows boarded up. She didn't plan on letting anybody in for the rest of the year.

In our series, The Adventures of the Bailey School Kids, we juxtaposed two elements not ordinarily linked to surprise readers and hopefully entice them into reading our stories. Here are a few of our titles to give you a better idea.

Vampires Don't Wear Polka Dots
Santa Claus Doesn't Mop Floors
Frankenstein Doesn't Slam Hockey Pucks
Ninjas Don't Bake Pumpkin Pies
Angels Don't Know Karate

Spend a few minutes making up your own forced relationship titles. Perhaps they will spark a story idea. After you've exhausted title possibilities, you're ready to move on to the ideas suggested on page 54. Have fun!

Time Lines

Remember the times of your life? Debbie's middle-school son recently had to make a time line of his life. This was an enlightening experience because it brought to mind so many different milestones in her son's life that she had forgotten about. Not only that, the activity provided a "lifetime" of topics that her son could write about.

Time lines can also be an excellent tool for a writer. Our lives are filled with emotional events that can provide us with writing topics.

Begin by listing all the important events in your life—the good and the bad. Think about the turning points, celebrations, and the catastrophes that make you who you are. After you have your list, organize them on a time line.

Begin with your birth or your first memory, and draw a line across the top of your paper. Label your time line with each year of your life, all the way to the present. For every year, list events that took place

TRY IT YOURSELF: TIME LINE

Try the following time lines. After you've completed the time lines, don't forget to spend a few minutes looking for writing sparks!
1. Your personal time line
2. The time line of a fictional character
3. The time line for one of your parents
4. The time line for a figure in history
5. The time line of a current leader

in your life that were important to you. (But don't worry if you don't remember events for each year. It's OK to skip years!) Perhaps there was an exciting vacation or the birth of a sibling. Maybe it was a move to a new town or the remarriage of a parent. It could be the day you found a bird that had fallen from its nest or simply the memory of completing a jigsaw puzzle with your father.

When you're finished take a hard look. Did one of those milestones stick out as particularly memorable because of how deeply it affected you? Did you believe at the time you would never get over the pain? Then this is something you should write about. The things that are the hardest to write about will mean the most to you and your reader. Or maybe there was an event that you realize many people have experienced. Could this be a spark for a magazine article? Or maybe the emotional impact of a life event could be the beginning of a poem.

Here is part of Debbie's time line. (Now you'll know just how old she really is!)

1959	1960	1962	1963	1964	1965
• Birth.	• Moved to Indiana.	• Brother was born.	• Got Lady, our dog.	• Moved to Henderson.	• Started school. • Good friend Doug was stabbed by a pencil in school.

Marcia tried the same activity. Take a look at a few of her life's memorable events.

1963	1965	1966	1967	1969
• Moved to Kentucky and couldn't get into kindergarten. • Fell and had to have five stitches in my head. • Grandma sewed a special little pillow just for me.	• Dad let me get a kitten that I named Nutmeg. • My sister and I found Nutmeg dead on the street on our way to school.	• Dad's car broke down on the way to school, and I thought it was my fault since I begged him to take me to school.	• A group of bullies terrorized me during recess until one of them stood up for me. We became best friends. • Mom and I spent summer evenings taking long walks.	• I got a guitar for Christmas. • Dad and I would sit at the kitchen table playing guitar and singing folk songs. • My best friend got a guitar, too.

Did you see any sparks in our lives? We found a few!

1. An article focused on caring for new pets
2. An easy reader about playground bullies
3. A novel with a character who has a musical family
4. An article for kids who are moving to a new community

5. A poem about a new baby in the house
6. A memoir about any of the events

If you're planning to write fiction, another time line you should try is a character time line. Make up a character and events in that character's life. You may come upon a gem of an idea hidden in your character's life. For example, let's create a time line for a character named Molly.

Age 1	Age 2	Age 3	Age 4	. . .
• Molly learns to walk.	• Molly chokes on a bone and almost dies.	• Molly's sister, Angie, is born.	• The kids at preschool make fun of Molly's thumb-sucking.	• And we could go on and on until we come to an idea that really sparkles.
	• Her mother becomes overprotective.	• Molly starts sucking her thumb for attention.		

Possessions

This strategy is related to time lines, but it focuses on priceless possessions instead of events. List items you've collected, especially the ones you'd never consider getting rid of. Look in that old box you've carried from house to house, or the box your mother gave to you when you moved out.

Here's Marcia's list.

★ Cedar chest
★ Writing desk
★ Little pillow
★ Silver dollar
★ Teddy bear
★ Raggedy Ann doll
★ Pearl ring

Listing your valuable items is the easy part. After you've completed your list, take the time to choose one and write its story. Marcia got so involved in this activity she ended up writing memoirs about her dad's silver dollar, her teddy bear, and the cedar chest that her dad gave her mom!

Possessions also spark fiction ideas. Look at Marcia's list again. Can you think of a story in which all those items become important? Try writing a character description for someone who owns those possessions. How does it change the story if the character is a boy instead of a girl? If the character lived in 1882 instead of 2000?

TRY IT YOURSELF: POSSESSIONS

Now it's your turn. Use possessions to spark your writing.

1. List your most valuable possessions.
2. List your parents' priceless possessions.
3. Kids are great collectors. They collect feathers, stamps, rocks, books, and arrowheads. Interview kids to find out what possessions they find priceless.
4. When you're alone at your writing desk, review your survey findings. Then ask yourself, "Why?" Why might feathers be worth collecting for a story character? Why would a box of stickers be worth fighting over? Why would a character hide three stones she found in a dried streambed? Why are postage stamps collectibles?
5. Write descriptions of possible characters who collect the things on your lists.

Doodling

Do you scribble, sketch, or doodle when you talk on the phone or listen to a speaker? If so, you have already practiced this story spark. If you're not a doodler, the time has come to try it out. Many people consider doodling a waste of time, but that is not necessarily the case. One of the most creative minds of all time, Leonardo da Vinci, considered doodling "a new device for study which, although it may seem trivial and almost ludicrous, is nevertheless extremely useful in arousing the mind to various inventions." Leonardo referred to studying stains and coming up with ideas from those stains. The same thought can work with doodles or scribbles of your own making. Debbie's idea for a new book about a circus Mama evolved from this doodle. The triangles became the circus Mama's dress.

TRY IT YOURSELF: DOODLING

Try the following activities to get your noodle into doodling.

1. Close your eyes and scribble on a piece of paper. Open your eyes and write the first thing that comes to your mind.

2. Call a friend and talk to her for at least five minutes. During the entire phone call make yourself scribble. After you say good-bye take a look at your scribble. Study it for a few minutes and see what pops into your mind. Write at least two sentences.

3. Feel like being a famous artist today? Get some paint and blob it on a piece of paper. Fold the paper in half and open it back up. Look at your paper—what does it bring to mind? Write a short paragraph.

4. Have a stamp pad handy? If not, borrow one and make thumbprints on a piece of paper. Go wild and connect the thumbprints. Now, give those thumbprints names and a history. What's wrong with that messy one anyway? Do you like the characters you've created? It could be the basis for a story.

5. Sketch from memory a place that you liked as a child. Now, describe that place in writing. How did you feel in that place? What did you do there?

6. Quickly sketch a character from your story.

7. Re-read your favorite poem. Capture the "color mood" of the poem using watercolor splashes.

8. Make an annotated sketch for the nonfiction magazine topic you're considering.

In My Shoes

Several years ago, we went to a workshop, and during the weeklong program, novice writers went to sessions provided by well-known writers. Pam Conrad led one session that Debbie attended. Pam asked everyone to close their eyes and focus on their main character's shoes. Are they scuffed and soiled? Are they brand-new? Perhaps your character is even barefoot. Doing this exercise helped Debbie realize she was telling her *Cherokee Sister* story from the wrong perspective. Debbie rewrote her story from a white girl's point of view, with the girl wearing the shoes Debbie had imagined.

TRY IT YOURSELF: IN MY SHOES

1. Close your eyes and think of a character. Try to imagine that character in front of you. What type of shoes is your character wearing? Don't rush. Let your mind tell you about this character through his shoes.

2. Close your eyes and try the first exercise again, but this time don't stop with the shoes. Visualize the entire outfit your character is wearing. Clothes can tell you a lot about your character's personality and time period. However, clothing is not everything. Does your character have dirty fingernails? Is every hair in place, or are there enough tangles on your character's head to trap a lion? What about scars? How did she get that scar on her knee?

Musical Muse

In our busy worlds it's often hard to take a break from the rush, rush of our everyday lives. But that is exactly what we are suggesting here. Put on soft music and lie on the couch. Listen for at least five minutes. Does the music bring anything to mind? Experiment with different types of music to see what each arouses in you.

TRY IT YOURSELF: MUSICAL MUSE

1. Try doodling as you listen to music. Do you see a story start in your doodle?

2. Try making a list as you listen. Jot down whatever crosses your mind.

3. Listen to music that was popular when you were young. What were you like then? Can you imagine yourself in your childhood bedroom when you were young listening to this music? Jot down your memories.

Summary

We hope the exercises in this chapter have taught you one thing: There is no need to fret when faced with a blank page, because the strategies in this chapter can get you sparking toward a fantastic story.

Use brainstorming to let your mind go wild and come up with ideas you never even imagined. Forget the rules for a while and be as creative as possible. If those ideas haven't sparked the great American novel, picture book, article, or poem, try listing and questioning.

We believe the most successful writers are the most stubborn ones. They don't give up on themselves or on their ideas. So don't give up if research isn't the answer for you. Everyone is different and is sparked in different ways. Perhaps you just haven't overheard the right conversation or read the right letter yet.

The powerful thing about the strategies in this chapter is that they can be combined. Try the brainstorming technique with the five senses. Then try webbing and listing. Don't give up. The best ideas seem to come with work, so plug away a bit longer than you think you should. Let your idea simmer and come back to it with a fresh mind.

All of the activities in this chapter can be used over and over again, so redo your favorite activities to see what else you can add to your idea collection.

Here is the most important tip in this entire chapter: Write, write, write. Don't read so much that you don't write. Don't spend all your time doodling or making time lines or listening to music. They are all good strategies, but that's all they are. They are activities to help you get started and, in some instances, ways to further develop your writing ideas.

The preceding methods are not to be substituted for writing. Writing is the key. Make yourself write. After that, convince yourself to write even more. It may be hard at first, but the more you write, the easier it becomes. (Don't worry if you hate those first few minutes each day when you get started. That's pretty common.) Soon you will be surprised to find yourself thinking of characters and plots, topics and images, descriptions and dialogues without even trying. You will hunger to find a few precious moments in which to jot down those sparks.

And when you need to write, that is exactly what you should do. Write!

CHAPTER 3

A FAMOUS AUTHOR
ONCE SAID . . .

Hurrah! You've sampled the strategies in chapter 2 and learned that they're great tools to help spark your writing. But you are probably worried that your ideas aren't developing into real stories. How do authors come up with stories? Paul Brett Johnson admitted that "ideas are everywhere, but ideas are not stories. Stories that work must strike a chord at an intuitive level. Listen to that inner voice."

Marion Dane Bauer said that "to find good story ideas, you must understand what makes a story. A story involves someone who has a problem he must struggle to solve or who wants something he must struggle to get. (Character and plot are inseparable. As has often been said, plot is simply character in action.) The important word in that definition is struggle. If your character isn't struggling—if he's simply sitting around looking at, thinking about his problem the way most of us do in real life—you don't have a story. So to find a good idea you first have to find someone whose problem or desire feels compelling to you. Then you have to carry that someone around with you long enough to begin to know how he or she will solve his problem."

One of the most effective ways to discover a story is to pay attention. Joel Strangis suggests that "ideas are in you—they are around you—but you have to listen. Sit down, turn off the television, turn off the radio, turn off the CD player. Now listen. Who did you meet today? Yesterday? What did you do? Start writing. Ideas will come—if you will listen."

But what do you listen for? And where do writers go to listen? In this chapter, published authors will tell us where their story ideas really come from. Then, in the following chapters we'll use what we've learned to breathe life into your ideas until they're full-fledged stories.

Experiences and Memories

We've all heard the advice, "Write what you know." We're not sure we really believe that. After all, Debbie's never had a werewolf to dinner and Marcia has never had tea with a vampire. Yet we have written successfully about folkloric characters. But, we have to admit, writing about what you know does lend authority to your writing. More importantly, your personal experiences can be a treasure trove of story ideas.

Charlotte Herman admits she "likes to write from experiences, from memories. I look back and remember people, places. They all come back to find themselves in a story! As I write, they might change along the way, and I don't always know where the story will take me or how it will end. But I do know when it begins."

Many writers find stories directly related to a personal experience. Eve Bunting told us that she discovered her idea for a picture book after receiving a flyer in the mail about a museum's Butterfly Day. Participants received a larva and instructions on making a butterfly house. "Then those of us who had our own lovely butterflies would meet and set them free," she said. "I was the only non-six-year-old in the program! It was a wonderful experience that I turned into my picture book, *Butterfly House*."

Jane Yolen wrote *Owl Moon* because her husband took their children owling when they were little. "My husband is the original of Pa," she told us, "though he actually has a beard. The little girl in *Owl Moon* is not me but is based on my daughter, who is now an adult with her own daughters."

Often, experiences can be combined into one story. Nikola-Lisa told us that his idea for *One Hole in the Road* "came from two very different, but related sources." Day after day, he drove his third-grade daughter to school. And day after day, they noticed a pothole. The pothole "got bigger and bigger each day—taking over a full lane of traffic. This started me on the road to a manuscript about a hole that gets out of control." As Nikola-Lisa was working on his story, something else happened. "A construction company accidentally smashed a hole in a seawall," he said. "That caused the Chicago River to flood the underground storage areas beneath Chicago's downtown Loop area. Putting both events to-

TRY IT YOURSELF: EXPERIENCES AND MEMORIES

Use experiences and memories to spark story ideas.

1. Remember experiences you've had. An old photo album or year-book may encourage memories.
2. Interview family and friends about their experiences. Not only will you walk away with story ideas, but also you'll learn to appreciate the people in your life even more!
3. After you've collected a list of experiences and memories, examine them for story ideas. Which ones do you find compelling? Use strategies from chapter 2 to help you develop stories. Ask "What if?" Try webbing for details. Write dialogues for the people involved in the memory. Freewrite.

gether, I came up with the finished manuscript, *One Hole in the Road*."

Experiences don't have to be your own. Story ideas can develop from experiences and memories shared by those close to you. Marion Dane Bauer's book, *On My Honor*, is based on something that happened to a friend when they were both about thirteen.

Eileen Spinelli found an idea for a picture book after a snowstorm threatened to cancel church services. "One Saturday night it snowed," Eileen told us. "By Sunday morning snow had drifted against doors, had buried cars and bus-stop benches. The pastor of our church at the time was away on study leave. The guest minister called the pastor's wife to say he would not be able to make it through the storm. Some church members suggested she cancel the service. But she would not hear of it. She prepared a brief prayer service. She put on her boots and coat and hat and scarf. She waded through the snow to the church. She lit the candles in the small side chapel. She turned on the heat. Barnabus, the church cat, arrived. So did three or four other people—and my idea for *Coming Through the Blizzard*."

OK, now it's your turn. What experiences and memories have you had that can be turned into a writing piece? What experiences have others shared with you? Jerry Spinelli suggests that struggling writers try visiting their own past. "You are sitting on a mountain, or at least a hill, of stories," he advises. "Be alert: Ideas don't often trumpet their arrival. They are nipping at us all the time; we're just not paying attention. One day I reached into the fridge for my fried chicken to take to work. Only bones were left, but I saw more. During lunch hour that day, I combined fact (chicken bones) with imagination (putting myself in the place of the culprit who ate my chicken) and wrote the first page of my first published book, *Space Station Seventh Grade*."

Don't worry if your memories don't sound like exciting stories. If you're writing fiction, you can turn any experience into a fun story by asking, "What if?" That's what we did after that infamous bad day with the students in our school. Marcia told Debbie they'd have to grow ten feet tall, sprout horns, and blow smoke out their noses just to get the kids' attention. Neither one of us actually turned into a vampire, but we got a great story by simply saying, "What if a group of kids *did* get a teacher who was really a monster and could grow horns and fangs?"

The Great Big World

You don't have to have a lifetime of exciting experiences to be a writer. There are other people out there making stories even while you are sitting quietly in your cozy home. In fact, there's a great big world full of stories. Just open your eyes and ears to discover the stories unfolding.

One of the best sources for ideas is the news. Jane Yolen found ideas for two of her books in the news. She began writing the Commander Toad books after seeing a newspaper article about a boy and his frog. "They had just won a jumping-frog contest," she told us. "The frog's name was Star Warts. I thought it would be funnier if the frog had been a toad, since the old superstition is that toads give you warts . . . so I invented frog and toads in space on a ship called Star Warts."

Armageddon Summer was inspired after reading about a group declaring the end of the world. "These news stories pop up every year," Yolen said. "I began noodling—that's a writer's technical term for thinking about a subject as a possible book project. I asked myself: What if a teenage girl is dragged to a mountain top by her family under the influence of a religious millenialist cult and meets a teenage boy also brought up the mountain kicking and screaming. Would there be a summer camp romance? Would they be Romeo and Juliet, dying at the end? Or would the whole cult go down, like the Titanic? I remembered my novel idea every time a new crazy cult—led by a Jim Jones or a David Koresh—hit the news. Then one day I called my best friend Bruce Coville. And I said, 'How would you like to write a book together?' "

Jerry Spinelli suggests writers "read the newspaper, especially fillers and back pages." Two of his best-selling novels, *There's a Girl in My Hammerlock* and *Wringer*, were inspired by newspaper stories. "In

66

TRY IT YOURSELF: THE GREAT BIG WORLD

During the next week, read your newspapers and magazines twice. First, read them like you usually do. Then, go back through them looking for embers that can be fanned into a story.

1. Read the obituaries. Yes, it sounds a bit morbid. But obituaries are about characters—real-life characters.

2. Do the same with the wedding and anniversary announcements.

3. Search for articles that imply human drama; stories that suggest real people struggling to succeed—or survive. Natural disasters like tornadoes, hurricanes, and fires cause heroes to surface. Cowards, too.

4. Pay attention to stories of conflict. Not only obvious conflicts, like wars and shootings, but hidden conflicts as well, like zoning proposals and announcements of new shopping centers.

5. Read the paper with a child's eye. What might need more explaining for a child to understand? Could a nonfiction article or book be developed to help kids make sense of a topic?

6. How might the headline topics concern kids? The development of a new mall might be great for adults. But what will it do to the empty field where neighborhood kids look for arrowheads? The fact that a local park has become a place to pick up a date means one thing to parents, another thing to teenagers, and something totally different to a nine-year-old who wants to play baseball.

---

each case," he said, "I took a basic fact or two and layered them with story and character."

Paul Brett Johnson was inspired while reading a personal-interest story in his local newspaper. "The story featured a woman who took in stray cats—lots of them. I got to wondering what the neighbors thought." Those thoughts led to the story, *Mr. Persnickety and the Cat Lady*.

The world is a great big place, and there are magazines devoted to showing us all its wonders. Jerrie Oughton was enjoying leafing through her new *National Geographic Magazine* when she found a story idea buried in an article on cave art. "In the article," she explained, "there was a brief mention of a cave drawing showing the story of First Woman and how Coyote foiled her attempt to do a good deed. It is a Navajo legend. As I sat on the sofa and thought of the story, the words came to me almost in the form of a poem. I kept in mind Native American traditions while using sparse words to tell the tale of *How the Stars Fell Into the Sky.*"

Newspapers, magazines, news shows. They're full of stories—stories waiting for you to discover them!

Things Kids Care About

It's true that kids today are different than kids of the 1800s. New technology provides more opportunities and experiences. But are young readers really that different? We don't think so. Kids are kids. And most kids have the same concerns.

When we visit schools to do writing workshops, one of the first things we ask student writers is, "What do kids care about?" As we discussed in chapter 1, the lists might vary, but usually they're similar no matter what part of the country we're visiting. Even more, they're similar to the types of things that *we* cared about when we were their age. They care about school, homework, teachers. They long for trusting relationships, acceptance, popularity, and loyal pets. They fear rejection, humiliation, and the loss of family.

Things kids care about are a good place to start looking for sparks.

Robert Kimmel Smith knows that the things kids care about in their everyday lives make for good stories. He recommends working in a school where you can talk with kids. "When you have gained their confidence," he suggested, "ask the kids what's the worst thing going on in their lives. Good conflict makes for good stories."

He knows, for instance, that kids care about their rooms. "We live in a big old house, built in 1910," Smith said. "One night, out of the blue, my ten-year-old son told me he loved the house, loved his room, and he *never* wanted to live somewhere else. I felt good about this, but it made me think of how territorial kids are about their home space. And an idea came unbidden. 1) A boy loves his room. 2) Boy loses room (I had no idea how or why). 3) Boy fights like crazy to get room back. Two years later I wrote the book *The War With Grandpa*, which has won a dozen prizes and is in its twentieth printing."

R.L. Stine, popular author of the Goosebumps series, admitted that he doesn't write from actual experiences. According to an article published in the Southern Kentucky Festival of Books program, Stine said he "never turned into a bee—I've never been chased by a mummy or met a ghost. But many of the ideas in my books are suggested by real life. When I write, I try to think back to what I was afraid of or what was scary to me, and try to put those feelings into books."

TRY IT YOURSELF: THINGS KIDS CARE ABOUT

1. Interview kids you know. Make a list of the things they care about.
2. Remember when you were a kid. What were your worries? Concerns? Wants? Make a list.
3. Look over your lists and choose three that appeal to you. Now, write the description of a fictional character who is worried about one of the items on your list. Use another concern to develop a nonfiction self-help article or informational book. Use the forced relationships strategy from chapter 2 to write a poem about the third idea from your list.

We've worked in schools as teachers and writers for years and witnessed the kinds of things that concern kids. Many kids are very competitive. They see winning as a type of approval. We used that idea for our Triplet Trouble series. *Triplet Trouble and the Field Day Disaster*, *Triplet Trouble and the Cookie Contest*, *Triplet Trouble and the Pizza Party*, *Triplet Trouble and the Bicycle Race*, and *Triplet Trouble and the Red Heart Race* all center around the theme of competition.

Most kids experience having a pet at some point in their life. If they don't have a pet, they want one. Pets can cause all sorts of concerns for kids. Beverly Cleary's *Henry Huggins* is a classic story about a boy who wants to keep the stray dog named Ribsy. Our book, *Triplet Trouble and the Runaway Reindeer*, explores the worry that occurs when a pet is missing. Marcia's book, *Godzilla Ate My Homework*, shows what happens when a character can't control his pet and lands in trouble.

Family, pets, friends, rooms. Think like a kid, and you'll find the characters, conflicts, and places that make up a good story imbedded in everyday life.

The School Connection (Curriculum-Based Ideas)

Where do kids spend most of their time? You guessed it: School.

Gone are the days when curriculum-based books were dry and didactic. Now, librarians and teachers look for books that bring their curriculum alive, making their students care and understand.

Fiction series like the American Girls series and the Dear America series are two examples that successfully make the school connection. Nonfiction series are being used throughout classrooms as well, and

TRY IT YOURSELF: THE SCHOOL CONNECTION

Try making the school connection to spark your writing.

1. List all the school subjects you remember.
2. Interview a teacher about subjects she covers throughout the year. Add her suggestions to your list.
3. Search the local library or bookstore to see how many books you can find that would support a school connection. Add these related topics to your list.
4. Look over your list. Is there a school connection you could make?
5. Could you make an analogous connection between a school topic and kids' real lives?

---

many magazines are making the school connection. Magazines have the advantage of being published in a timely manner, and teachers find that they support the curriculum effectively. *Cobblestone*, *Dolphin Log*, and *Zillions: Consumer Reports for Kids* are three magazines that teachers are using to supplement their curriculum.

Examining subjects taught in school can lead to interesting writing ideas for you. Becoming familiar with school topics may spark a few ideas. School topics haven't changed much. Students still learn about celebrations, explorers, habitats, and the history of their country.

Debbi Chocolate's first book was written after searching in vain at the library for a book just like it. According to Chocolate, "there weren't any books like the one I was looking for. So that night, I went home and wrote a story called *A Very Special Kwanzaa*, about an African American boy celebrating the Kwanzaa winter holiday. Because there wasn't a book like it, my story was sold and published right away."

Joel Strangis got the idea for his second book while working at a school. Strangis told us that "according to local legend, the school had been a station on the Underground Railroad. I researched those legends. Although the legends weren't true, I found out many other interesting things about the Underground Railroad, and soon I had the outline for my second book, *Lewis Hayden and the War Against Slavery*."

Parallel thinking can help you turn big ideas, world events, and complex issues into kid-sized story ideas. War is a horrendous but important part of our history. How can you write about volatile events for children? One way is to make your big idea analogous to something in a kid's life.

The war in Vietnam was a pivotal point in American history. Lines were drawn and the nation was torn in two. Marcia used parallel thinking to help develop a story set in 1968. While the nation squared off over draft dodgers, a group of kids in her story, "Truth or Dare," discover there are different types of courage during a go-cart competition that lands one of the characters in the yard with two vicious dogs. Should he run away or fight?

Writing to Remember

Maybe you had a grandmother who rode to her wedding in a wagon or an uncle who hitchhiked across the country during the depression. Was your aunt's piano covered with black-and-white photographs of people you never met, but wanted to? Where did that antique cedar chest in your mother's room come from? Our families' histories sparkle with story gems. We only need to take the time to record the stories.

Charlotte Herman told us that a photograph sits on her piano. "It was taken in 1914 and shows my five-year-old mother, her two sisters, and their mother and father (my grandparents). I've always been mesmerized by that picture, and whenever I looked at it I'd recall the stories my mother told of growing up in a one-room house in a small town in Russia. 'Can you imagine,' she asked, 'that at one time there were eight of us living in that one room? We had a curtain that divided the room. On one side was the kitchen, on the other side was the bedroom.' She spoke of the soldiers who came to make their investigations. 'They investigated what you had and if they wanted it they took it.' I knew I had to write about that small house, and the town, and the people who lived there. So from that old picture, from those memories shared with me, came my book *The House on Walenska Street*."

Most of us aren't lucky enough to know the whole story. Instead, we grow up hearing only snippets of family stories. But don't let that stop you from using them as story sparks.

Marie Bradby used part of a family story to write her picture book *The Longest Wait*. Marie told us that the book "is a fictionalized story about my grandfather who got caught up in a snowstorm while delivering the mail in the Knickerbocker Blizzard of 1922. I wrote this book so that my son would know this family story. I come from a large family. In the summers on Sunday evenings, my aunts, uncles, and cousins would come visit and we would all sit out on the front porch eating vanilla ice cream and orange sherbet. My uncles and my mother often would talk about the past, including my grandfather's (their father's) journey. I was intrigued and always wanted to know more. When I

TRY IT YOURSELF: WRITING TO REMEMBER

Use your family history to spark your writing.

Spend an afternoon looking through old family photographs. Find pictures that make you curious about the people and setting.

1. Interview parents and grandparents about their lives as children.
2. Look back into your own childhood. Was there a neighbor that kids feared? A stray dog that terrorized the playground? A new child from Romania who couldn't speak English?

became an adult, I realized why they could tell me only so much. They were very young children at the time of the incident. That got me to thinking about them as children. What was it really like for them to wait for their father to return home? How did they bear through his illness? And were they also anxious to go out and play in the snow? This book is a story about patience and faith. While researching and writing it, I realized that my family story was part of a larger public story. There were many families whose lives were changed by the blizzard."

We agree with Marie. We're all part of a larger public story. That larger story may include legends and folktales.

Joel Strangis's first book was based on an Italian folktale told to him by his mother. "When she wrote it down," Joel said, "it was less than 100 words. I expanded it, added characters, scenery, and dialogue, and voila— I had a 1,500-word picture book story called *Grandfather's Rock*."

Where Did They Get Their Ideas?

Writers are such nice people! We asked fellow authors to share the story sparks for one of their books and suggestions for generating the idea. Their responses were as unique as each individual writer, but as you will see, most authors use a combination of strategies to spark their stories into life. Their responses are scattered throughout this book, but in this chapter we focused on the inspiring stories of how they got their ideas. We've already discussed some, but here are even more. We hope you find their anecdotes as interesting and helpful as we did.

Marion Dane Bauer

Author of *On My Honor, If You Were Born a Kitten* and *An Early Winter*.

Usually my ideas don't come from real life. Or they may start from real life—a newspaper story, an incident that happens to me or to one of my friends, something odd one of my pets does—but from there they go into my imagination and become something very different. What is essential, always, is that I must be able to find a central place where I can feel whatever it is that the main character feels. It is because of those strong feelings that my story, if it works, makes you feel strongly, too.

Marie Bradby
Author of *The Longest Wait* and *More Than Anything Else*.

My writing tends to come from two areas. One, I have fictionalized several stories. I started writing them in order to explain them to myself, and to pass them on to my son. In these stories, I have tried to tell my son things about life—past and present—that I believe are important. Writing has to address the most important questions that you can think of at the time. Family stories are who we are. We need to keep them alive. Two, occasionally stories will drift into my head as if someone is talking in my ear, telling me what to write down. I call these "gift" stories. They can be about characters that I don't know and places where I have never been. I have gotten several entire stories this way, but often the gifts come as a line or two, and I have to figure out the rest.

The hardest part is making yourself ready to receive and recognize the gift story. For me, it takes a certain physical and mental space from routine and chores. In fact, most of these have come to me when I was away from home, relaxing, and not thinking about writing at all. The subjects tend to be something that my mind has been processing for years, even decades. I am not usually aware that this processing is going on. All that practice writing is helpful at this stage. I use the writing skills that I have honed and just go with it.

I keep a journal. I'd like to tell you that I write in it every day, but I don't. What I do write in it is my life and tidbits of things that happen in the world around me, news or overheard conversations. For me, reading literature, news stories, and nonfiction are the best ways to get the pen going. I will read something, especially poetry, and it will strike a chord with me that centers on truth. I can read just two words of something that really touches me and a character and situation will pop into my head.

Now, I don't usually have problems with generating ideas, I have problems with finishing—carrying the idea through to the end with all the necessary elements of fiction, such as beginning, middle, and end. I get stuck with, "What will the character do next?" I need ideas to keep going with what I have started. After I get the pen going again, I am

OK, unless of course, I go off on a totally new tangent. Then I have a new story that I have to see to the end. I think I see new stories while I am working because of my training as a journalist. Years ago, a fellow reporter told me that when you go out on assignment, always look for a new story that you can work on after you finish the first story. I think that training has made me aware of the "next story," which is essential to a career as a writer.

Marlene Targ Brill
Author of *The Trail of Tears: The Cherokee Journey From Home* and *Let Women Vote.*

My daughter was six years old and none of her teeth had fallen out. Since her friends were losing teeth already, she was most disappointed. She wanted to leave her teeth for the tooth fairy. Being the good parent, I tried to find books about the tooth fairy that might make her feel better. What I found back then were few books that were truly fun. I wondered: Where did the idea of the tooth fairy come from? And do children everywhere leave their teeth for the tooth fairy? These musings led to research that wound up being *Tooth Tales From Around the World*, the only nonfiction history of the tooth fairy.

Clyde Robert Bulla
Author of *The Chalk Box Kid*, *A Lion to Guard Us*, and *Shoeshine Girl.*

I saw a girl working in a shoeshine stand—first shoeshine girl I'd ever seen. Maybe an idea for a book, I thought. I stopped for a shine. The girl was learning. The shoeshine man told her, "I'm going to shine one of his shoes. You watch what I do, then you shine the other one." The girl had difficulties, but I liked the way she tried. I gave her some money. She looked at it as if she had no idea why I'd given it to her. The man said, "That's your tip. You didn't earn it, but you can keep it." All this gave me the start of a story. Later, when I went back, the girl was gone, but she had grown in my imagination, and she became the heroine of my book, *Shoeshine Girl.*

Eve Bunting
Author of *The Wall*, *Night of the Gargoyles*, and *The Blue and the Gray.*

Be interested in everything around you. Watch and listen. Only write about what moves you emotionally. Carry a notebook and pencil so you can capture a special place or a special feeling that may not come again.

I clip articles from the newspaper that interest me. I write down sayings that seem to be filled with a hidden wisdom or humor and save those, too. I pay attention to what is happening in the world around me.

Debbi Chocolate
Author of *On the Day I Was Born, A Very Special Kwanzaa,* and *Imani in the Belly.*

Listen to the funny things your friends, or parents, or little brothers and sisters say. Observe them closely and keep a notebook of the funny ways in which they act or behave. There are plenty of funny things to write about right in our own circle of family and friends if we look closely enough.

My favorite strategies to generate ideas are to talk with younger children and to spend time with younger children to learn what they like to read about and what their interests are.

Joy Cowley
Author of *Singing Down the Rain, Red-Eyed Tree Frog,* and *Big Moon Torilla.*

Ideas are sometimes triggered by rich sounds. For example, one cold wet day I was dreaming in a steaming, scented bathtub, murmuring the word, "wishy-washy, wishy-washy." Suddenly, a cow and a pig and duck and a crazy woman jumped into my head and wrote their own story. It seemed that *Mrs. Wishy-Washy* came from nowhere. But stories never come from "nowhere." Behind it all was the Saturday night bath for a family who lived in a house without electricity. Water was boiled over a fire and poured into a tin tub. My two sisters and I were then scrubbed by our mother who had a rough washcloth in one hand, a bar of yellow soap in another.

I believe that most children's writers write directly, or indirectly, from their own childhood.

Sid Fleischman
Author of *Jim Ugly, The Whipping Boy,* and *By the Great Horn Spoon.*

Skimming through some book of folklore, I came across the old belief that one born at midnight had the power to see ghosts. Almost at once I saw the possibilities. If pirates had buried some treasure, together with their murdered captain, and then lost the map—they could find the spot again if they could spy on the captain's ghost pacing his gravesite. My young hero then would have been born at the stroke of midnight. Learning this, pirates would kidnap him, carrying him off to the island to spy the ghost and show them where to dig up the treasure.

One idea doesn't a story make. It takes two. Say a prince in love is turned into a frog. Second idea: princess is allergic to frog. Now you have a story idea to run with.

Mem Fox
Author of *Wilfrid Gordon McDonald Partridge, Whoever You Are,* and *Wombat Divine.*

My grandfather, Wilfrid Partridge, lived in an old people's home. When I visited him I noticed and mourned the lack of children. Old people and children get along brilliantly, yet here they were, separated from each other by the craziness of our society. So I decided to write a book that brought children and the elderly together in the hope that teachers would initiate similar contact.

My granddad never lost his memory. He was sparky and wonderful to talk to. I visited him weekly until he died suddenly of pneumonia at age ninety-six. That's why Miss Nancy in the book (*Wilfrid Gordon McDonald Partridge*) is ninety-six. The other old people in the book have the dignity and characteristics of the people who lived in the same home as my grandfather. "Mrs. Morgan" lived next door to him and played her organ for hours, crying from "melancholia." "Mr. Bryant" was very tall. "Mr. Hosking" wasn't an old person—he was one of my favorite colleagues.

Jacque Hall
Author of *What Does the Rabbit Say?*

I come from a large family who loves pets. My own four children and my ten grandchildren have owned every pet imaginable, including dogs, cats, ponies, horses, chickens, parakeets, and snakes. It wasn't until my oldest granddaughter received a rabbit as a gift that I realized a rabbit doesn't make a noise (except thumping). There is no vocal noise associated with a rabbit, such as "moo" with a cow. I thought to myself, "Ducks quack; cows moo; chickens cluck; doves coo; monkeys chatter as they play, but what does the rabbit say?"

Aha! That generated my idea for a picture book *What Does the Rabbit Say?* There are many picture books for young children relating to animal sounds, but I think mine presents a new slant.

Try thinking of a new idea and then writing the opposite of what the predictable would be. Listen to kids; read, read, read. Watch kids' shows on TV.

Ruth Heller

Author of *Chickens Aren't the Only Ones, How to Hide a Crocodile and Other Reptiles,* and *A Cache of Jewels and Other Collective Nouns.*

The information that spills over when I am researching for one book invariably sparks new ideas. The page of sargassum seaweed in my book *Plants That Never Ever Bloom* triggered the idea for all my books on camouflage—the How to Hide series of books and also for the book on which I am currently working about the Sargasso Sea.

Read! Read! Read! I do not think that anyone who does not read can write.

Charlotte Herman

Author of *Max Malone Makes a Million, The House on Walenska Street,* and the Millie Cooper series.

I like to write from experiences, from memories—from the inside out. I look back and remember people, places. They all come back to find themselves in a story. As I write, they may change along the way. I don't always know where the story will take me or how it will end, but I do know where it begins.

Smells bring back memories: a box of crayons, freshly sharpened pencils, and a brand-new school year is starting for me. Songs and sounds and old 8mm movies. Everything stirs those memories. The memories find their way into my stories.

There are objects that need no memory associations—only imagination. Once at an antique show I saw an old wagon. A tin box was attached on the underside. I could only wonder: Who did this wagon belong to? Who or what did that child have in the wagon? A friend? A dog? Newspapers? And what was hidden in the box? Where did the child live? In the city? On the farm? So many questions. Now to search for answers.

Esther Hershenhorn

Author of *There Goes Lowell's Party.*

I attended, for the first time ever, a Folk Art Festival in Evanston, Illinois. Struck by a booth's display sign, "Steven Shelton, Limner and Fancy Painter," I spoke with Steven and had a mini-lesson on the history of itinerant portrait painters (which is what limners are) prior to the discovery of photography in 1848. Steven gave me book titles, painters names, various and sundry resources. It turns out that he, at the ripe age of twenty-six, was living the life of an 1840s limner and fancy painter, traveling the United States, staying in people's homes and painting their portraits, harpsichord covers, and walls. I bought one of Steven's beautiful painted boxes, took his card and said, "Steven Shelton, you are my very next picture book, *Fancy That!*" I could "see" the story and pictures. Now, had I not stopped by that Folk Art Fair . . . well, who knows what book I would have written next.

Will Hobbs
Author of *The Maze, Ghost Canoe,* and *Far North.*

I get ideas from my own life experiences and from reading, probably about half from each. The more personal experiences a writer has to draw on, the broader the range of things he or she has to write about. Go places, do things, meet people, have a lot of interests, keep building up that well of experiences you can tap into when you face the blank page. I also read widely: novels, nonfiction, newspapers, magazines. I love to clip out articles about interesting, quirky, unusual things. I have files and boxes I throw clippings into, and when I'm in my wool-gathering stage, I'll rummage through all of these materials.

In addition, it helps me to prewrite, to make notes in my computer about possible characters, possible plots, little events I might work into a story. I call this file my "ponies," and I picture them running wild off on the horizon, raising dust. As I get closer to starting a new story, I picture myself "visiting" each of them, calling to them, seeing which one might be ready to run with me.

Joan Holub
Author of *Boo Who? A Spooky Lift-the-Flap Book, I Have a Weird Brother Who Digested a Fly,* and *What's the Magic Word?*

While at the library, listening through the bookshelves (I was on one side in the stacks and mom and child were on the other side—I never saw them), I overheard a child ask his mom why she and dad got Mother's and Father's day, but there was no "Kid Day" just for him. Mom said, "What about your birthday," and he said, "What about yours?" I was at the library researching ideas, and this gave me the beginning of *Happy Monster Day.*

Paul Brett Johnson
Author of *The Cow Who Wouldn't Come Down, Farmers' Market,* and *Old Dry Frye.*

Ideas are everywhere. But ideas are not stories. Take an idea—any idea—and use free association to stretch it into a story. Ultimately, the stories that work must strike a chord at an intuitive level. Listen to that inner voice.

I keep an "idea box." When something presents itself—an interesting character, an intriguing situation, a fond memory, an anecdote in the news media—I make a few notes on a $3'' \times 5''$ card and put it in my idea box. Occasionally I sift through these ideas to see if a story line comes to mind.

W. Nikola-Lisa
Author of *One Hole in the Road*; *1, 2, 3, Thanksgiving!*; and *Bein' With You This Way*.

I think the most important thing is to be a good observer. I jot lots of things down that interest me, not because I think they'll make a book idea—just because they interest me. It's only later when I go through my notes that I sort and evaluate what I've collected. It's like trolling for fish with a giant net—you catch a lot of fish, many of which you throw back, and some you keep.

To tell you the truth, ideas are my strength. I'm never in want of an idea. The problem is knowing what is of value, and what to focus on. I think this in and of itself is an important strategy: to find out what your strengths and weaknesses are as a writer. Lean on your strengths, and try to develop your weaknesses. Because ideas are my strength I have a very intricate filing system for storing ideas, which I go through on a regular basis. It is from these ideas that I develop stories. Sometimes I'll carry an idea around for years until it ripens or some external event pulls it to the front of my attention. In other words, don't throw ideas away just because they don't work for you now. Someday they might be important and become the ground upon which you build a story.

Phyllis Reynolds Naylor
Author of *Shiloh*, *Sweet Strawberries*, and *Alice on the Outside*.

I had no intention of writing a book about cats until one of our two cats, Ulysses, swallowed forty yards of Christmas ribbon, eleven rubber bands, as well as grass and hair, and who knows what all. The operation to relieve him of indigestion cost $450, and I swore I was going to get that money back. So I wrote a book about two cats, Marco and Polo, and the mysteries of life as viewed through a cat's eyes. I'm happy to say that I got my money back many times over. To write a book from the point of view of a cat, of course, you have to "become" a cat—to think like a cat, walk like a cat, stretch like a cat. It helped that my editor was looking for a good anthropomorphic book, so everything came together at about the same time for *The Grand Escape*.

Start with something deep inside yourself to generate ideas. Try to remember the most embarrassing thing that ever happened to you, the angriest you have ever been, the most frightened, or the most sad. Write only a few sentences about it, and then turn it over to your imagination and add a new ending, a new beginning, new characters, until the real and the imaginary blend into a whole new story. Another gimmick, if your idea cupboard is totally empty, is to think up a common stereotype—canary: a small, cute, yellow, sweet, beautiful little bird—and change just one thing about it. Example: the world's most ferocious canary. Let your imagination do the rest.

The more you write, the more you will see stories in things you never considered worthy of writing about before.

Joan Lowery Nixon
Author of *The Haunting, Who Are You?*, and *A Family Apart.*

Newspapers are a terrific source of ideas, which grow into plots. A few years ago, on vacation in southern California, I read a feature in the Sunday edition of *The Los Angeles Times* about a man who threw elaborate parties, traveled extensively to Europe, and had no visible means of support, even though he was obviously wealthy. His neighbors, who assumed he must be a drug dealer, were astounded when he was arrested for art forgery. I saved the clipping, followed up by researching art forgery and art theft, and before long the idea for *Who Are You?*, my 1999 young-adult mystery novel, was born.

Wendie Old
Co-author of *Busy Toes.*

Picture rain like you've seen this year. Picture darkness. Picture three tired writers in a Caravan taking the Pennsylvania turnpike—and the Caravan starts hydroplaning. Picture the driver turning into a close-by (thank heavens) rest stop to get her nerves back. Deep breath. Start again—out on the Pennsylvania turnpike, dodging trucks, and handling hydroplaning.

Picture the writer in the backseat asking, "What do you do with toes?"

The other two say, "Huh?"

"What can you do with toes? All I can think of is digging in the sand."

Driver gets a glimmer that the writer in the back seat (now to be revealed as Claudine Wirths) is trying to get our minds off the terrible driving conditions by giving us a writing problem. By the time several ideas about doing things with toes are tossed about, Driver tosses her purse into the back seat.

"Write these down," Driver says. (Driver is yours truly). "In my purse there is a small flashlight, pens, and a notebook." (Okay, I'm a mom. I carry lots of emergency things in a large purse.)

We spend the rest of the trip thinking of things to do with toes.

To make a long story sorta short—yes, this is how *Busy Toes* was created.

We each tried to do something with the list. Decided the picture-book idea was the best one. (Meeting at a Chinese restaurant halfway between our three houses, where I brought fifty different types of newly published picture books to illustrate what various publishers were looking for in picture books.)

Then we polished the text by E-mailing it back and forth.

And, it sold—after being sent to ten or fifteen publishers by the third of this group, Mary Bowman-Kruhm.

Busy Toes is published under a pseudonym, which includes parts of all three names: C.W. Bowie.

Jerrie Oughton
Author of *How the Stars Fell into the Sky, Music From a Place Called Half Moon*, and *The War in Georgia*.

Read poetry. It's like an antihistamine for clogged brain passages. Read a lot. Meditate and remember. Begin with the earliest memories you have and remember your life. Play the word game of description: in your head, describe things or people you see. Work crossword puzzles to keep the words flowing. Daydream. It's time well spent. Cut off the TV and find spaces of quiet time. And . . . never give up! What one loves with passion will finally come.

I read certain extraordinary books, sometimes over and over again. I never waste my time reading something that isn't in some way uplifting.

Richard Peck
Author of *Strays Like Us, A Long Way From Chicago: A Novel in Stories,* and *Don't Look and It Won't Hurt.*

Once in a while a valued writing colleague jogs you into action. Harry Mazer called on his fellow writers to contribute gun stories for his anthology, *Twelve Shots*. I haven't squeezed off a round since basic training, but I thought Harry could use a comic short story with a female central figure. I wrote "Shotgun Cheatham's Last Night Above Ground" for him and then showed it to my book editor. She thought it might work up into a novel composed of short stories. It did. It became *A Long Way From Chicago* and won a Newbery silver medal from ALA. Thank you, Harry.

Befriend librarians, particularly school librarians, who can tell you what young readers are actually reading.

Do not "bounce" your ideas off fellow adults. You're not writing for them.

Listen every day for authentic young voices. The one voice your story doesn't need is yours.

Remember that your readers remember no decade before the 1990s, no president before Clinton. And be warned: What you remember best about being young probably never happened.

Robert Quackenbush
Author of *Batbaby, Daughter of Liberty: A True Story of the American Revolution*, and *Two Slapstick Biographies: Once Upon a Time! A Story of the Brothers Grimm and Quick, Annie, Give Me a Catchy Line.*

A number of my author/illustrated books were inspired by our son, Piet, when he was growing up. When he took his first steps, at age one, he set out to prove he could fly as well and went crashing to the floor off a sofa. I thought it was time to tell him about the Wright Brothers, so I wrote and illustrated my first humorous biography *Take Me Out to the Airfield: How the Wright Brothers Invented the Airplane*, which has led to twenty-three more over the years.

Piet continues to be an inspiration for new books. He recently graduated from Emory University, where he majored in history, and he has joined the working world. My latest books reflect on that theme of venturing from home and striving for independence. *Batbaby* is about the adventures of a baby bat going on his first solo flight. Another book, *Daughter of Liberty*, is about courage, patriotism, and determination, all necessary to become successful in an uncertain world.

For me, writing and illustrating involve the same process, which is observing other people and their experiences. I am involved in a lot of activities where there are children, including the after-school art classes that I offer at my studio three afternoons a week and giving presentations about my work to schools and libraries. Children's interests change from week to week, and it is important for me to be where they are to generate ideas.

One of my favorite strategies that I use for generating ideas is to seize a phrase I have overheard and build on that. I will grab my trusty yellow pad and a pencil and start writing with that phrase in mind. "A roach in the kitchen" led to a book about a duck named Henry who literally demolishes his house trying to get rid of an ant in his kitchen in *Henry's Awful Mistake*.

Pat Rynearson
Author of *The Bandage Bandits, Elephant Upstairs*, and *The Talking Lizard*.

All children seem to go through a stage where they love bandages. My three boys were no exception. We went through a period of years where we never had a single bandage in the house because I could not buy them fast enough. Every tiny bump or scrape needed several bandages. My two younger sons carried it even further and had bandages on dolls, toys, furniture, and everything else they thought had a "boo-boo." I started calling my boys "The Bandage Bandits," hence the title of my very first book.

Keep a journal every day. Clip interesting articles from newspapers and magazines so you have an idea file you can refer to when you get stuck. Use freewriting. Just start writing anything that comes into your head and see if it doesn't get your juices flowing. Brainstorm with friends, family, and colleagues for ideas. Jot down favorite family anecdotes and stories. They can be great jumping-off places.

I write a lot of multicultural stories. I start by going to the library to research the country that I am interested in. Many of the books have photographs of children from the country. I find a child whose photograph really jumps out at me. Then I imagine myself as that child and what my life would be like if I were her or him. What would my day be like? What food would I eat? What would my house be like? And most importantly, what do I dream of?

I also keep a title file. Many times I will hear a phrase or saying and I think to myself, "That would make a wonderful title for a book." So I write it down and put it in my file. I might not know what the story is about right then. But I can go back to it. Sometimes I will write a line or two along with the title to remind me what I was feeling and thinking when I wrote it down. I have just completed my story, "The Washerwoman," whose title I wrote down seven years ago!

Jerry Spinelli
Author of *Knots in My Yo-Yo String, Wringer*, and *Maniac Magee*.

Often the title is the last thing to arrive. With my short novel *Fourth Grade Rats*, it was the first. I remembered an old schoolyard chant: "First-grade babies/Second-grade cats/Third-grade angels/Fourth-grade rats."

That last line struck me as such a natural book title that it had to be used. I wrote it at the top of a sheet of paper and made up a story to go along with it.

Martha Bennett Stiles
Author of *Island Magic*.

I vacuum. Stall mucking is also pretty good, but less widely accessible. Weeding is good. Do not think I am being flippant. What these activities share is that they don't take much mental concentration; your mind can float or roam around. Also, you are doing useful work. You are not sitting feeling tenser by the minute because, lacking an idea, you are doing nothing, you are a failure, you are untalented, stupid, doomed. Nothing of the sort. You are cleaning the house (or barn, or garden). The assurance will relax you, as will the physical exercise, and ideas come best when one is relaxed.

Joel Strangis
Author of *Grandfather's Rock* and *Lewis Hayden and the War Against Slavery*.

The ideas are in you—they are around you—but you have to listen. Sit down, turn off the television, turn off the radio, turn off the CD player. Now listen—who did you meet today? Yesterday? What did you do? Start writing. Ideas will come—if you will listen.

When I sit down at my computer, the first thing I do is play a game for five to ten minutes (no more) to separate my writing from the rest of my day. This helps me concentrate and open me up for ideas.

One final note—go to a bookstore—a big bookstore. Look around. All those books and all those magazine articles were written by real people, just like you. Most of them are no smarter than you and many are not as smart as you. But they listened to the voice inside themselves, then they sat down. They wrote, and they rewrote, and rewrote, and rewrote, and. . . .

Anastasia Suen
Author of *Delivery*, *Window Music*, and *Baby Born*.

Here is the story behind *Toddler Two*.

I walk every day. It's my quiet time, my thinking time. Most days I "write" while I walk, too. I write in my head. I don't bring any paper with me. I think that's why it works. No paper means no commitment, so my mind is free to go, and find something wonderful.

I am a rewriter. I take books in and out of the drawer. I write them.

I rewrite them. I send them out into the world, and if they come back too many times, I rewrite them again. On this particular day, I had taken out a book about a toddler's day. I had tried to sell this book many times over the years, but it wasn't working. No one would buy it. I'll rewrite it, I thought. What could I change? Nothing came to me when I was sitting in my office, so I went for my walk.

Three blocks away, by the oak tree, it came to me. These words just popped into my head, "Toddler, toddler, toddler two, two is the number just for you." A counting book! I was writing a counting book. Good-bye, toddler's day. I kept walking. Suddenly, I could see my old Mommy and Me class. My fifteen-year-old was two again. I could see the mothers and the children. We were doing finger rhymes with the children in our laps. That was it! A finger rhyme! Hmm . . what came in twos? Eyes, hands, feet?

By the time I finished my miles, I had the entire book written in my head. I repeated it over and over to myself, so I wouldn't forget it, and when I came home, I wrote out the first draft right away. I did more fine-tuning the next day on my walk, all without paper, and when at last the book was ready, I sent it out into the world. Five weeks later, I had an offer.

"Don't give up" is my motto. I am a stubborn writer. I write every day and I keep writing. I rewrite constantly. I am going to be published one way or another. I keep writing until something works.

The flip side of that coin is, "Let it go." If an idea isn't working, if a book is stuck, I put it back in the drawer. I let it wait for another day. I let my subconscious work on the book. I give myself lots of quiet space, and time to think. I trust myself.

"Don't give up" gives you a prepared mind. You write every day, so you think like a writer. "Let it go" allows you to tap your intuitive side, and make connections, to think deeply. Use them together to develop your craft and write words that have layers of meaning, words that touch the heart and the mind.

Examine an idea from all sides. Explore it fully. Create mind maps. Write back story. Think about your idea before you go to sleep at night, and write down what comes to mind upon waking. Journal. Set your kitchen timer and write until it rings. An idea is just a seed. How it grows is up to you.

Glennette T. Turner
Author of *Running for Our Lives, Follow in Their Footsteps,*
and *Take a Walk in Their Shoes.*

Some neighbor children gave a surprise party for their mother. They involved all the families on our block. A year or so later, when students in my classroom learned that I was going to take a leave, they began to plan a surprise party for me. Both parties were total surprises and made the honorees very happy. I combined these along with a few fictional touches to write *Surprise for Mrs. Burns*.

One suggestion to help struggling writers is to draw a web and write keyword(s) in the center (it is most productive if the keyword is linked to a relationship or event that made a great impression). Next, I ask lots of what-ifs and jot down my answers.

To generate ideas, observe situations from different perspectives. Explore/jot down answers to "what if" questions. Keep a journal. Record thoughts and feelings along with facts. Ponder in the shower. Ask lots of questions. Listen carefully.

Natasha Wing
Author of *Jalapeño Bagels, The Night Before Easter,*
and *The Night Before Halloween.*

I got my idea for *Jalapeño Bagels* from a recipe book. I was helping a friend assemble a local bakery's recipe book and read their introductory story about the owners. One owner grew up in a multicultural family— Latino and Jewish. I imagined what the owner looked like as a seven-year-old boy and placed the story in their bakery. I used one of the flavor bagels the local bakery makes as the title and solution for my story. The bakery was kind enough to let me use two of their recipes in my story.

Audrey Wood
Author of *The Napping House, Birdsong,* and *Bright and Early Thursday Evening: A Tangled Tale.*

My first memories are of Sarasota, Florida, in the winter quarters of Ringling Brothers' Circus. I was one year old and remember it vividly. My father, an art student, was making extra money by repainting circus murals. The people in the circus were my friends. I was bounced on the knee of the tallest man in the world and rocked in the arms of the fat lady who could not stand up. My first baby-sitters were a family of little people who lived in a trailer next to ours. They told me stories about the animals they worked with: Chi Chi the Chimpanzee, an elephant named Elder, and Gargantua the Gorilla. I have used several of my circus experiences as inspiration for children's books.

Pay attention! Notice the story lines that play out in your own life experiences. When you tell a friend about an event in your life, think about the details and decide which ones could be discarded without changing the story. What happens if you plug other characters into the same story? Does it change? Is it better? Worse?

I collect ideas from many places—life experiences, dreams, things that interest me. I put my ideas in a huge box and call it my idea box. I refer to the idea box many times during each project, sometimes getting ideas that change the story dramatically.

Jane Yolen
Author of *Owl Moon*, *Wizard's Hall*, and *The Emperor and the Kite*.

I am always asked where I get my ideas from. That is a very difficult question to answer, since I get my ideas from everywhere: from things I hear and things I see, from books and songs and newspapers and paintings and conversations—and even from dreams. The storyteller in me asks, "what if?" And when I try to answer that, a story begins.

Editors' Advice
Diana Capriotti (Random House)
I prefer to edit middle-grade and young-adult fiction. Within those genres, good stories feature a character who readers can relate to in situations that are readily identifiable. Whether an author is exploring a contemporary issue, a historical event, or a fantastic voyage, strong characters and an honest voice are the strength behind writing for these readers. My advice for aspiring writers is to know your story, love your characters, and write from the heart. The best stories are lovingly crafted, but writing is also hard work, so put in the time rereading, revising, and rewriting to make sure you are constantly growing as a writer.

Tonya Dean (Guideposts for Teens and Boyds Mills Press)
Be very flexible and trust your editor to know what's best for his or her publication. Write with excellence: sharp, clean, fresh language with few (if any) errors. Be willing to do WIT (whatever it takes) to polish your writing—even if that means several drafts.

Caitlyn Dlouhy (Simon & Schuster/Atheneum)
I personally look for something that hasn't been done before and stories that speak from the heart. Ideas that kids relate/connect to, things they themselves experience, are always attention-getters.

Write about what you know—that usually adds an enthusiasm to your writing that shines through to the reader. Don't jump on the latest trend. By the time you do that, several books on that trend will already be in the works.

Helen Perelman (Hyperion Books for Children)

A good idea is the starting point. It is a start of a story, a character, a plot, or even a scene that inspires the writer to begin. Writing for the market is tricky. While I think that writers should be savvy and know what kids today are interested in and relate to, I do not think that people should cater to only those interests. Most importantly, the story has to mean something to you as the writer. If you are writing simply to get published, you are missing the process of writing. Write because you enjoy writing, not because you want to be published.

Becoming market savvy requires the writer to do a bit of research. Watch kids and more importantly *listen* to kids. What are they talking about? How are they talking? What interests them? Spend some time in the bookstore or online at Amazon.com, taking notice of the best-selling books. Visit schools and see how kids choose books to read and how they go about reading. Take notice of what toys, games, movies, and television shows capture kids' attentions.

In paperbacks, there is a range of types of stories that we publish. There are teen books, fantasy, science fiction, humor, middle grade, chapter books, and young chapter books. I like to work on a variety of paperbacks.

Write because you enjoy writing. Don't worry about getting your story published or finding an agent until after you have completed a manuscript. Research the publishing houses and see where your story would fit in. Publishing houses look for different elements in the books they choose to publish. You need to be able to wear a marketing hat as well as your writer's hat in order to sell your book to an editor. You are the start of the marketing chain. Once you sell the book to the editor, the editor needs to sell it to an acquisition board and then to a sales force. The sales force then needs to convince a book buyer to buy the book for the store. The "selling" starts with you, the writer. No one knows your book better than you, so start doing research and finding the right house for your story.

Summary

The wonderful authors and editors highlighted in this chapter prove that story sparks are everywhere. We hope you keep reading because in the next chapters we tackle taking the ideas we've gathered from chapters 1 through 3 and begin shaping them into stories.

IGNITING THE SPARKS

Fantastic! You've done the "Try It Yourself" writing exercises from chapter 2 and sparked more ideas from fellow authors in chapter 3. You've filled three hundred journals—or at least several pages—with possible ideas, but none of them resemble a story. Now what?

The ideas you've generated so far are like the parts to your car's engine. Standing alone, they just look impressive. But add the spark that ignites the gas and those individual parts rev into action and your car takes off. To spark your writing engine, we'll consider each part to make sure we have everything we need. After we've polished those individual parts, we'll talk about sparking them into action.

This chapter will help you focus your ideas into story material. Reflecting on the elements of fiction and nonfiction is an excellent way to help writers spark the actual writing process. We'll begin by taking a look at these writing elements. Then we'll review the writing process so there won't be any surprises when you sit down and devote valuable time to your writing.

Exercises along the way will help you collect all the material you need to spark your engine, rev into high writing gear, and take off!

Fiction Elements

There is so much to consider when you write a fiction piece. It's good to have knowledge of what makes a story. Reflecting on the individual story elements can also help you develop potential ideas.

Six major elements are basic to every story. Let's take a look at each and see what sparks we can make.

STORY ELEMENTS

Character	Who is this story about?
Setting	Where and when does this story happen?
Conflict	What problem must the character solve?
Climax	What crisis forces the character to either succeed or fail?
Resolution	How has the character changed or grown?
Plot	What happens in this story? Why and how do they happen?

Character

Character answers the question: Who is this story about? In his book *Fiction Is Folks*, Robert Newton Peck, author of the popular Soup books, told his readers that "When the question is 'What am I going to write about?' the answer is 'Who?' "

Many writers believe all stories develop from the characters and their actions to prevent—or reactions to—a problem. In other words, a story begins when you take a person and plunk him down in the middle of a situation to see what he does. Characters drive the story. Without the character, nothing of interest would happen. It is through characters' eyes, ears, words, behaviors, and emotions that the reader is led through the story's events to a satisfying conclusion.

There are basically three types of characters to consider. The protagonist is the main character in the story. This is the character with whom you want the readers to identify; the one for whom you want them to root and want to see succeed. The antagonist is the adversary of the main character; the character who complicates life for your main character. The other characters are secondary characters. They're the people who fill the life of your main character; the people with whom he or she interacts on a daily basis.

The characters in children's stories are often regular kids who find themselves in unusual predicaments. There's a good reason for that. Readers want to relate to the people they read about. It allows them to live the story's events vicariously through the well-drawn characters, and it enables readers to build an emotional bond with the characters.

If readers can't relate to the story characters or don't like the characters, they may not bother to finish your story—especially emergent readers still struggling with reading. They have to really care if they're going to invest so much effort when they could be playing soccer or watching television. That's why it's very important for writers to devote time to developing strong characters.

Another reason you'll want to consider the characters is that your characters will help define story events. Different people act in different ways. Through their actions, we learn about their beliefs, motives, and abilities. For example, if you have a character who you've shown as brave and daring, that character wouldn't naturally run away from the school bully on the playground. If he does, it will seem unbelievable to the readers. Certain types of characters will behave in certain ways, so spend time getting to know how your character might act.

Another important aspect of character development is dialogue. People have specific styles of speaking. We learn about their personalities through what they have to say and how they say it. The same is true for the characters in the stories you plan to develop.

Finally, remember to really get to know your characters and their thoughts. That's the only way to develop well-rounded people who won't come across as one-dimensional or clichéd.

When planning to write for children, limit the number of characters and vary the characters' names. Make sure each name is as different as the characters' personalities. Reading a story about Rob, Randy, and Ross can be difficult even for the seasoned reader.

Character Activities
How many characters can you create? Use the Create-a-Character chart on pages 92–93 to help you create realistic characters.

Setting
Some writers insist that stories are built from characters. Others argue that stories must start with setting.

"When I start a story," Jerrie Oughton told us, "I start with place. Characters come out of setting. In *Music From a Place Called Half Moon*, I knew the story would take place in the mountains where our family cottage was. From place came my characters."

Setting identifies the place and time during which your story evolves. It answers the questions: Where and when does this story happen? Naturally, the place and time will affect the behavior of the characters and how the story's plot develops. Simply put, you can't have

CREATE·A·CHARACTER

Name

Age and grade level

School name

Teacher's name

Hair color

One distinguishing physical feature

One distinguishing personality feature

One physical habit (e.g., drumming fingers)

One speech habit

Hobbies

Family members

Pets

Thing of which he/she is most proud

Thing he/she hopes nobody will ever find out

Strengths

Weaknesses

CREATE·A·CHARACTER

Fears _____

More than anything, the one thing he/she wants _____

_____

His/her idea of the perfect way to spend a summer day _____

_____

The best part of school _____

The worst part of school _____

The name of his/her best friend _____

The one thing worth fighting about with his/her best friend _____

_____

Prized possessions _____

_____

When is his/her birthday? _____

Has he/she ever had a birthday party? When? What was it like? _____

_____

Where does he/she live? _____

What's hanging on his/her bedroom wall? _____

_____

your Revolutionary War drummer boy call his mother on the phone to let her know he's OK! That's obvious. But it may not be as obvious that your suddenly homeless protagonist from downtown Chicago easily survives in the wilderness of Michigan, or that your pioneer boy readily befriends a Native American hunter. When developing stories, keep in mind the setting and how it has defined each character. Character and setting are interrelated, and together they help build your story.

Setting can also be an integral component of your plot, even becoming an antagonist for the main character to face. An excellent example is Karen Hesse's *Out of the Dust*, the 1998 Newbery-winning book set in the midst of Oklahoma's Dust Bowl during the depression. The dust storms and depression era become protagonists against which the main character struggles. Another example is *Across the Wide and Lonesome Prairie* by Kristiana Gregory, a title in Scholastic's popular Dear America series. The unsettled western environment provides plot events that character Hattie Campbell struggles against as she travels the Oregon Trail.

When you're writing for children, it's imperative that you write about a kid's world: backyards, playgrounds, the woods at the edge of the neighborhood. Limit the setting to places where kids spend their time. Even then, it's easy to find yourself in the rut of seeing surroundings from an adult's perspective. As writers, we need to suspend our adult view and look at things like young readers might. When developing the setting for stories, pay particular attention to the details you include. Are they really what a kid would notice? Look at the following example to see what we mean about the differences between an adult's and a child's perspectives.

THE MALL

Adult's View	Kid's View
Price tags	Sneakers and other kids
Exorbitant prices	A balloon on the ceiling
Grumpy clerks	The man who forgot to zip up his pants
Crowds	A store that sells bubble gum
Sale signs	Half-eaten cookie on the floor

Knowing the setting of your story will allow you to develop believable details and plot events. When it comes time to write, it's not necessary to bore readers with lengthy setting descriptions. Instead, describe only enough to make readers feel they are in that place, especially if you are working on historical fiction or science fiction. Rely on showing your characters naturally interacting with just enough of their environment to

TRY IT YOURSELF: SETTING

1. Take a writing field trip. Experience a movie theater, forest, shopping mall, playground, and swimming pool using your senses. Visit these settings and jot down what you see, feel, hear, smell, and taste.
2. Use a chart like the one shown on page 94 in some of your favorite places. What's the adult view of the location? The kid's view?
3. Where and when would you like to be? Go to the library and/or use the Internet to research an interesting time and place. List details that would help define a character and that might interest a reader.
4. Plop one of the characters you brainstormed in the character section of this chapter into different settings. Write brief descriptions showing how the setting would affect the character. Remember: Setting will influence dress, speech, actions, and beliefs.

give readers a sense of place and time. Readers need to be able to "see" the setting to believe your story and relate to the events as they unfold.

Conflict

Conflict is a problem with which your main character must struggle. It answers the question: Will he/she ever get out of this mess? Without conflict, there really is no story. Look at the following example to see what we mean.

Thelma ate her cereal and then brushed her teeth. " 'Bye, Mom," she yelled as she grabbed her pile of books and slipped out the door. The birds were singing and bright daffodils poked up out of the yards she passed on her way to school.

"Do you have your homework?" Mrs. Beckham asked as soon as all the kids were seated.

Thelma passed her homework forward and smiled. She knew that every one of her math problems was correct.

By the end of the day, Thelma had finished all of her work. She even had time to help her best friend.

That night, Thelma did her homework. She remembered to floss her teeth before crawling into bed. It had been a perfect day.

Unfortunately, a perfect day for Thelma does not make for a perfect story. There is nothing at stake to hold the reader's interest. A good story needs to include drama and suspense to keep readers turning the pages. Let's look at Thelma's day again and see if we can give it a little drama as an example of how important conflict is in your story.

Thelma ate her cereal and then brushed her teeth. " 'Bye, Mom," she yelled as she grabbed her pile of books and slipped out the door. The birds were singing and bright daffodils poked up out of the yards as she headed to school.

She was almost to the school. She just had to get past the stretch of sidewalk that wound through Dedman Forest. The towering trees reached their bony branches high overhead, blocking the sun's warmth as Thelma hurried through the woods. Not far away a bird screeched, and she was sure she heard something rustling through the tangled vines. Goosebumps raced across her arms. She hugged her books to her chest and ran until she reached the other side of the woods.

Sweat trickled down her forehead and her heart hammered in her chest. Thelma stopped to catch her breath.

"Whew," she said to herself. "I'm glad that's over."

Just then, a giant shadow covered the sidewalk. Thelma looked up at the sky. There, hovering right above her head, was a dragon coated with scales as green as the leaves in Dedman Forest.

Thelma stumbled back, dropping her books to the ground. The dragon's wings hummed as it stretched its neck down close to Thelma. She barely breathed as the dragon darted around her. When it was done looking her over from head to toe, the dragon turned and shot a stream of flames right down at her pile of books. Before it disappeared into the forest, the dragon looked back at Thelma and slowly winked one yellow eye.

Thelma raced to school, barely making it to her seat before the bell rang.

Mrs. Beckham looked at Thelma's messy hair and frowned. "Do you have your homework?" Mrs. Beckham asked.

Thelma held up her charred piece of paper and gulped.

See what a little conflict does for a story? When something is at stake and there are obstacles for the character to overcome, readers will keep reading.

96

TRY IT YOURSELF: CONFLICT

1. Examine some of your favorite books for children. List the major conflicts of each.
2. Take one of the setting activities you completed in the last section. Brainstorm problems that might arise from the environment.
3. Choose one of your characters from the character activities. Brainstorm conflicts for the character. The character attributes that describe things your character is willing to fight for are particularly good for brainstorming conflicts.
4. What if . . . ? Brainstorm a list of "what if" situations for one of the characters you have developed.
5. Kids are your best resource. Interview a group of kids about problems kids face. Clyde Robert Bulla told us, "One strategy is to visit classrooms. When I ask them what kind of book they would like me to write, they tell me."

Take time to consider conflicts when planning a story. Choose one that will keep kids interested until the very end. Perhaps there is a struggle with another child or bully like Debbie's *King of the Kooties*, or maybe it's a struggle against nature as in Gary Paulson's *Hatchet*.

Story Climax

The climax is the apex of your story where the conflict is somehow addressed or resolved. The climax answers the question: What crisis forces the character to either succeed or fail? It's the dramatic turning point in your story where your character either succeeds or fails; the all-or-nothing scene. The climax is what everything in your story has worked up to, and it's what your readers have hung around for. Don't disappoint them! Make the climax the most severe crisis in your story and write so dramatically that readers won't be able to put the book down until they find out what happens.

In children's books, the child protagonist must be the one to complete the struggle. An exception to this is in picture books where the protagonists may be adults, especially in fairy tales, legends, and tall tales. But if your story centers around a child protagonist who has been battling a school bully, for example, it's a cop-out if that character has the conflict resolved when the principal catches the bully and has him transferred

TRY IT YOURSELF: STORY CLIMAX

1. Examine the ending scenes of your favorite books. Write a brief summary of them next to the list of conflicts you listed earlier. Note how the climax scene involves the child protagonist and directly relates to the conflict.
2. Look at the list of conflicts that you brainstormed earlier. Write a summary of a climax scene for each conflict.
3. Don't be afraid to work backward. Think of an exciting climax (or take one from the exercise above). Build your story to fit your favorite climax scene.

---

to another school. That makes the principal the hero. Kids want to see kids being the hero, so make sure the child protagonist is responsible for solving the climax's crisis scene.

Resolution

The resolution is your story's ending. It is the point where the climax is resolved, and it shows the result of the main character's struggle. There should be no surprises at this point. No winning lottery ticket, no dream sequence. The resolution should be a believable and natural conclusion to the events that have unraveled throughout the telling.

The character has been through a great deal since the beginning of the story, and it's important that an apparent change occurs. That's why the resolution answers the question: How has the character changed or grown? In most fiction books, the climax results in the child protagonist being victorious. That doesn't mean the endings are always happy. The climax can result in a loss, as in *Prairie Songs* by Pam Conrad and *The*

TRY IT YOURSELF: RESOLUTION

1. Take out your list of favorite books where you've jotted down the conflicts and climax scenes. Look at those books one final time and note how the resolution ties up loose ends and shows the growth of the main character.
2. Using the list of characters and conflicts from the conflict section, brainstorm how the characters could change by the end of a story.

Yearling by Marjorie Kinnan Rawlings, but the hero or heroine has learned a valuable life lesson and therefore is made richer by it.

The time to end the story is as soon after the climax as possible. In brief, the character had a problem, it resulted in a struggle, there was a turning-point crisis—now it's over! Don't summarize, preach, or explain. The events of your story and the character's change should be all you need. In his book *Plot*, Ansen Dibell suggests writers "get the story down and then close the curtain as quickly as possible, while the reader is still halfway wanting more . . . don't dither. Avoid weak, throat-clearing closes, just as you'd avoid throat-clearing, inconclusive openings. Let the ending be the ending, without waffling afterthoughts."

Plot

Plot is everything that happens in your story. It is the sequence of events during which your main character struggles to solve a conflict. The plot answers the basic question: What is this story about? But it's not really that simple. Plot involves character, conflict, setting, and motive. It is the essence of your story and shows the how and why of unfolding events.

A basic plot has three major parts: beginning, middle, and end.

The purpose of the **beginning** is to hook the reader. From the first page, the reader should have an idea about what type of story he is reading, who the story is about, when and where it takes place, and with what conflict the character will struggle. If you can't do it on the first page, it should be evident by the end of the first chapter. It's a good idea to plop readers right in the middle of the story so they will feel compelled to turn that first page and keep reading (and so will editors).

The **middle** of the plot includes a series of scenes showing character actions and reactions that complicate the character's struggle. Ansen Dibell explains in *Plot* that "the job of a middle is to build toward and deliver crises. And since scenes are the foundation of fiction, the foundation of plots are special scenes, big scenes."

Everything included in your story must move the plot toward a major crisis. If one of your characters gets poison ivy, there needs to be a reason why poison ivy is important to the struggle.

The middle of your plot must move at a brisk pace or you run the risk of losing readers. Using hooks—scene grabbers at the end of chapters that compel readers to keep turning the pages—keeps readers involved (more about hooks in chapter 6).

The **ending** of the plot revolves around a crisis, or climax, during which the conflict question is answered. Either the character succeeds or doesn't. Even if the story doesn't end on a happy note, the ending still

TRY IT YOURSELF: PLOT

1. Review some of your favorite children's books. Write one-line plot summaries for each.

2. Write a series of plot summaries based on the conflicts brainstormed earlier. Try to state the story idea using only one or two sentences. It might help to start with: This is a story about. . . .

3. Use the following chart to brainstorm a string of causes and effects for a character based on one of the plot summaries from activity one. Make each reaction of the character cause an effect that was not quite what the character had hoped!

THIS IS A STORY ABOUT . . .		
Conflict/Complications (the problem and complications)	Character(s) Reaction (what the character does)	Effect of Reaction (what happens as a result)

needs to be satisfactory. It needs to tie up all the loose ends of your story.

Stories for children tend to be plot-driven. The entire focus of the story involves the character struggling to overcome an obvious obstacle. There isn't much room for straying from the basic premise of your story, or readers will get confused.

One way to help you plot stories is by using one sentence to answer the question: What is my story about? If you can say what your story is about in one or two sentences, then you have a real grasp of your plot. If you can't, you don't have a firm understanding of the story. And if you aren't sure, try to imagine what will happen to young readers trying to make sense of it. If you aren't able to tell what your story is about in two sentences, rethink what you really want your story to be about.

Another plotting aid is to develop a simple list of cause-and-effect events that build in intensity. Let's take a look at one of our books for an example.

THE BAILEY CITY MONSTERS #6: SPOOKY SPELLS

Conflict/Complications (the problem and complications)	Character(s) Reaction (what the character does)	Effect of Reaction (what happens as a result)
Issy brags that she will win the spelling bee.	Annie decides the way to beat Issy is by studying. She wants to win the spelling bee fair and square.	Her brother Ben argues that playing softball is more fun than studying.
Their neighbor Kilmer's great-uncle Nilrem arrives. He offers to help them with the spelling bee. Issy is rude to Nilrem and Kilmer.	Friend Jane is determined to get back at Issy to teach her a lesson.	Ben talks Jane into playing softball instead. Nilrem tries to play.
Nilrem speaks in rhymes and he hits softballs out of the neighborhood.	Jane suspects that Nilrem is a magician who can cast spells.	Ben laughs at Jane.
Issy overhears Nilrem's spells. She threatens to get the police.	Ben comes up with a plan to save Nilrem and the school spelling bee.	Ben invites Nilrem to school to help kids study the old-fashioned way. But Issy is rude to him and makes him mad.
Nilrem casts a happy spell on Issy to make her less grumpy. Issy starts giggling and can't stop. She giggles all through the spelling bee—even after the police arrive. She tells the audience that Nilrem used magic to help Annie win. The audience freezes. The police make their way toward Nilrem.	Annie grabs the microphone and admits Issy is right. She said Nilrem was her friend and helped her study so she could win the contest fair and square. She explains that friendship is the most powerful magic of all.	The police leave. Nilrem decides to become a teacher because he learned the best magic happens at school.

Nonfiction Elements

Writing nonfiction isn't complicated in the same way as a fiction book is since there aren't characters to follow throughout a series of events. But lively and creative nonfiction can be just as difficult to write. Nonfiction includes many types of books: how-to, biography, history, and science. No matter what type of nonfiction you might be interested in writing, keep in mind the elements of nonfiction as you develop your ideas. Reflect on the individual elements to help you brainstorm potential ideas.

NONFICTION ELEMENTS	
Beginning	How can I hook the reader?
Middle	How can I bring this to life for the reader?
Ending	What do I want to make sure the reader has learned?

These three major elements are basic to almost all nonfiction. Let's take a look at each and see what sparks we can make.

Nonfiction Beginnings

The opening is your opportunity to show readers how fascinated they will be if they continue reading about your focused topic. This brief introduction answers the question: How can I hook the reader? The beginning also gives readers a hint at what they are about to learn. There are several ways you can bring your topic to life in this brief opening.

⭑ **Anecdotal experiences** use a person's testimony or experiences to show the importance of your topic. Anecdotal accounts, written to read like fiction, work because they allow readers to relate to the topic on a personal level. Let's take a look at an example. Which of these openings do you think is more effective?

Tracy held her breath as she whizzed down the icy slope at forty miles per hour.

Or

Snow skiing is done on snow or icy terrain. Skiers can often reach speeds in excess of thirty miles per hour.

If you said the first example, then you see the value of anecdotal accounts. They are an excellent way to grab the reader's attention.

⭑ Starting with a **question** directed to the readers automatically involves the readers with your topic. Readers make a personal connection when you ask a question like, "How would you design the perfect science fair project?" Hopefully, readers will want to read on to determine if their ideas match yours.

⭑ **Scene descriptions** ask readers to envision a picture of your selected topic. The purpose of the scene is to encourage readers to imagine being in the midst of your topic. Having them sit in the space shuttle and feel the vibration of impending liftoff is an example of effectively using scene description to engage readers.

TRY IT YOURSELF: NONFICTION BEGINNINGS

1. Go to the library and grab a handful of nonfiction magazines and books. Analyze how the authors hooked the readers. Which did you think were most effective?
2. Brainstorm a list of nonfiction topics you find interesting. Looking through those magazines and books will help with this, too.
3. Ask a teacher if you can look at the textbooks kids use in his classroom. What topics interest you? Add those to the list you started in the second activity.
4. Look over your list of topics from exercises one and two above, and choose three of your favorite. Brainstorm at least three unusual slants to the topics that would narrow them into subtopics that kids might find intriguing.
5. Browse the card catalog at the library. Are there hundreds of books on your subject? Are there any? Look in *Children's Books in Print*. Are there any recently published books on your subject? Ask a children's librarian if there is a need for your type of book.
6. Select your favorite idea from exercise four above. Briefly research that topic until you have a fairly adequate understanding of it. Try writing several opening hooks for your selected topic. The following chart may help.

NONFICTION HOOKS

Anecdote: _____

Question: _____

Scene: _____

Statement: _____

⋆ A **startling statement** of fact is also an effective way to grab your reader. "Only one in 6,500 writers will ever get published" is a dramatic statement to make. It certainly catches the attention of wanna-be writers! The readers will stay hooked if the statement is followed by an engaging question like, "Wouldn't you like to know how to be that one?"

Nonfiction Middles

The body of your nonfiction piece is the time to share what you've learned during your extensive research. The middle of the well-written nonfiction piece answers the question: How can I bring this to life for the reader? As a nonfiction writer, be aware of the audience and strive to make the content lively and entertaining. If you spend too much time reciting facts to your reader, the information will just go in one ear and out the other.

There are techniques that will help you liven up your nonfiction writing.

★ Many kids are visual learners and most need to base new material on knowledge they've already acquired. Breaking up your text with lists, charts, and graphs can help kids visualize the information you're sharing.

TRY IT YOURSELF: NONFICTION MIDDLES

1. Using your favorite nonfiction ideas, list three important details or facts that would need to be included in a nonfiction article.
2. Try writing analogies that describe:
   ★ the height of a full-grown redwood tree
   ★ the weight of a rhinoceros
   ★ the length of the Oregon Trail
   ★ the time it takes to fly to Saturn
   ★ the size of the small intestines
   ★ how a telephone works
   ★ how a computer works
   ★ how the court of appeals operates
3. What types of charts, graphs, lists, and exercises could be included in books about:
   ★ cat nutrition
   ★ the equipment taken on the Lewis and Clark expedition
   ★ how Columbus navigated without a computer
   ★ how to grow an herb garden
   ★ the communication of bats in pitch-black caves

* How-to books can also make effective use of exercises and activities that help readers try out what they're learning as they read.
* Using analogies and imagery also helps readers see and understand by relating your topic to something else with which they're familiar. Make comparisons to things kids find in their everyday lives. Instead of just *telling* them that Hoover Dam is 726 feet tall, *show* them by comparing it to a football field or the length of a family van.
* Organize your information in a logical way that would help young learners easily grasp the content of your piece. This can be done sequentially for some topics, but for others it might require you to begin with easier related information and move on to the most complex. Writers of biographies and historical stories will more than likely proceed in chronological order.
* You don't need to tell the readers everything there is to know about your topic. In fact, that is probably not possible in a children's book. Instead, focus on the highlights and interesting details.

Nonfiction Endings

Once you've brought your topic to life and have finished sharing the interesting aspects of your research, it's time to wrap up the piece. This is when you answer the question: What do I want to make sure the reader has learned? A brief highlight of your topic's interesting aspects and a review of how your piece has benefited the readers are all it takes. The ending of nonfiction pieces should not be long; it merely encapsulates what you hope readers have gained by investing their time and effort in reading your book or article.

TRY IT YOURSELF: NONFICTION ENDINGS

1. Take a look at those magazines and books again. Examine how each author attends to the ending.
2. Go back to those favorite nonfiction ideas you've listed. Beside each idea, write a brief description of what you'd hope readers would learn from an article about each.

Summary

In this chapter we've discussed the six major fiction-writing elements: character, setting, conflict, climax, resolution, and plot. We've also focused on the nonfiction elements: beginning, middle, and ending. The activities have gotten your writing engines in high gear. We've equipped chapter 5 with some high-octane ideas to put all the elements into an organized form to help you win the writing race. Let's roll!

5

CHAPTER

THE WRITING PROCESS

As with any activity, there is a process for completing your writing. We have visited schools across the world and found one thing to be universal: Teachers are focusing more on writing, and the writing process is being discussed more than ever in the classroom. When we talk with students we often touch upon this five-step process for writing. This process is exactly the same whether the writer is five or fifty-five. The steps are thinking, writing, rewriting, editing, and publishing.

Thinking

Thinking could also be called "prewriting." Before you even put your fingers on the keyboard, you have to spend some time planning what you want to write. The first step is the most important, and it's the focus of this book. If you choose to write before thinking out a plan, writing will be merely an exercise. It takes a creative thinker to make the writing sparkle.

Planning often takes longer than nonwriters could ever imagine. This is the time when writers dig deep for an idea to develop. It is also the stage where that idea is shaped and thought through. Many writers say they never put their pencil to the paper until their entire piece has percolated and they've envisioned their story from beginning to end. Planning before the actual story writing begins can save the writer from wasted drafts and false starts.

Of course there are writers who admit they begin with just a speck of an idea and start writing; that that the idea is developed through the writing. Jerrie Oughton keeps an envelope stuffed with her ideas. After she comes up with a strong setting, main character, and a first line, she feels free to write in the character's voice. "It's almost like my characters tell me what to say, and I just write down what he or she tells me to," she told us. "I write my first draft to discover what the characters will do."

During this prewriting stage, research can help you clarify your central ideas and discover supporting details that will flesh out your writing piece.

When we plan our books, we use this first writing step to brainstorm details for the plot. We rely on a combination of the idea-sparking strategies discussed in chapter 2. We might interview readers or scribble down a web. Then we hit the library, our own books, and the Internet. We search for tidbits that will make our story more interesting and will help us shape the direction of our story. After all that, we sit down and analyze what we've thought through.

We organize our books into chunks—or scenes of action. For longer pieces, those scenes can be developed into chapters. For shorter pieces, the chunks of writing might also be scene changes or subtopics of your main topic. Breaking your big piece into smaller chunks helps you do two things: One, it helps you focus on developing each part of your piece fully and two, concentrating on one small piece keeps you from getting frustrated and giving up.

Our scenes are organized into a list of events that develops our fiction plot. We find this list or rough outline very helpful, especially when working with a partner. The outline gives both of us a map to follow, though we often take detours between the beginning and the end. Our outlines range from simply one or two sentences about what we want to happen in each chapter to a complex paragraph or two about each chapter. Sometimes our outlines have been almost one-fourth of the length of the completed book. Sometimes the outline needs to be changed to fit the way the characters have grown, and that's OK. (Look for more about outlining in chapter 7.)

And all this is done before we begin writing the actual book!

TRY IT YOURSELF: THINKING

1. Participate in an activity a child might enjoy, such as karate classes, bike riding, or playing baseball. Make a web about that activity. Does anything in the web spark your interest?
2. Take one of the settings from chapter 4. Go to the library and research that setting. Learning more about the place and the time period will help you bring your idea to life.
3. Sit in a dark room for fifteen minutes and let your mind wander. Think about your story and let your thoughts flow freely.
4. Do a menial chore such as washing pots or shaving, but let your mind dwell on your story. It's amazing what your mind will come up with.

Drafting

Writing. This is what it's all about, right? Well . . . almost. This next part of the writing process is where you finally get to draft all the ideas you've been thinking about. But it's only a small part of finishing that piece.

After you have your outline finished, you have formally completed the thinking stage. Next, it's on to the writing stage. For us, this is the fun part where anything can happen, and usually does.

There is a misconception that writers are "inspired" to write. We don't really believe that. Thomas Alva Edison said, "Genius is one percent inspiration and ninety-nine percent perspiration." We believe inspiration comes while you write. It's like a conversation with a friend over a cup of coffee. You don't just tell that person the things you planned to say before you walked through the doors of the café. Instead, as you sit and sip your java, your conversation meanders from one subject to another. Something your friend says stirs a thought, and before you know it you're blurting out a new idea. The same thing happens while you write. The characters act and react, and pretty soon you have a new idea forming. It's important to keep your mind open to those ideas as you write—even if it means veering away from an outline.

Don't be critical as you write. Treat this stage in your writing process like the freewriting described in chapter 2. Your goal is to get ideas down on paper. If you expect your piece to be perfect as you write, the only thing you will accomplish is frustration.

TRY IT YOURSELF: DRAFTING

1. Select one setting, one character, and one plot from previous activities. Write two pages and if you like the focus, make an outline to continue your idea. Here, the thinking and the writing stage will intermingle.
2. Select one character from a previous activity. Create a family tree for this character. Select several family members and write a paragraph about each one.
3. Find a comfortable spot in which to relax. Now . . . write.

You'll never get your piece written if you listen to your critic during this stage. So don't worry if your draft isn't perfect. In fact, most likely it won't be. But the writing stage isn't the time to worry about that. This is the stage to let go and have fun and write like crazy.

Rewriting

The next stage, the rewriting or revision stage, is the least favorite for most people. It is the third, but vitally important part of the writing process. This is where you change and improve the content. Jerrie Oughton finds this a critical stage in her writing. After completing the first draft, she "reads what my characters have said and I look to see how I can enhance the plot. It is during the revision that I see what the story is really about."

A critique group—a gathering of writers whose goal it is to help each other grow as writers—can be very helpful at this stage. Sharing your stories with others helps you see your story through others' eyes. For more about critique groups, see chapter 8.

Rewriting can be painful when you really love your story, but almost every story can be improved through revision. It's often a good idea to let a story "simmer" a few days before you take it out to revise. Waiting allows you to distance yourself from your story so you can take a fresh look at it.

A simple but effective trick is to read the story out loud. Reading the story aloud lets you listen to the sound of the language and identify parts that don't make sense or sections where the words don't flow well. None of us want our readers to stumble over our words. We want our readers to concentrate on the great story we've written, so we try to make our words flow easily and naturally. The parts that don't sound quite right when read aloud are probably the sections you want to work on more.

Rewriting is not fixing periods and quotation marks. We're not to that stage, yet. Rewriting is looking for ways to develop your plots and characters to make them more realistic. Rewriting involves ensuring that your piece makes sense and that the writing builds toward an ending that will satisfy the reader. Rewriting concentrates on making sure the reader feels that she is actually in the place you've described. Revising is when you concentrate on honing the content by elaborating, combining, modifying, restructuring, adding, and deleting. Let's try an example. Read the following paragraph. How would you revise it? What would you change? Delete? Reword?

> The goat snorted and bent its head down. The two horns on top of its head were pointed right at Howie as it started running quickly right at him.

Here is Debbie's rewrite:

> The goat charged Howie.

Of course, Marcia calls Debbie the slasher, because she likes to cut unnecessary words. Sometimes it's nice to leave in a little description to add flavor. So this is Marcia's rewrite:

> The goat snorted and pawed the ground. Its horns pointed straight at Howie.

Which rewrite you liked will depend on what type of writer you are. But why did we change our original paragraph? Let's take a look at the first sentence: "The goat snorted and bent its head down." This is a descriptive sentence that helps set the scene, but it's not absolutely necessary and it's too wordy.

What about that second sentence? "The two horns on top of its head were pointed right at Howie as it started running quickly right at him." We deleted "on top of its head" because where else would a goat's horns be? "Started running quickly right at him" had to go for several reasons. First of all, running quickly is redundant. Use of the word "started" should be checked. It usually is not needed. (Everyone has pet words that they often throw into their writing without even realizing it. Deb-

REVISING CHECKLIST

Does the writing make sense?

Will the beginning catch the reader's attention?

Are the characters believable?

Is the dialogue natural?

Delete the adverbs. Use strong verbs instead.

Delete unnecessary words: "just," "seems," "some," and "like."

Has the main character changed or grown by the story's end?

Is there a variety of sentence structure and length?

Is there enough action?

Are pronouns specific? (Is it confusing who "he" is?)

Is the verb tense consistent?

Is the point of view consistent?

Does the writing "show" instead of "tell"?

bie's word is "just." So she writes her story, then goes back and rewrites her story without the "justs.") You also need to beware of the redundant use of a word—in this case, the word "right." Why did we substitute "charged" for "started running quickly right at him"? "Charged" is much more descriptive and shows the action precisely.

Years ago an editor took a writer in hand and walked him through the rewriting process. This rarely happens today. So where can a writer go today for help in revising his work? Critique groups can be lifesavers,

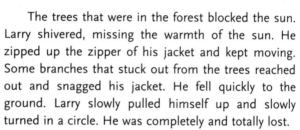

TRY IT YOURSELF: REWRITING

1. It's your turn. Try your hand at revising the following paragraph.

The trees that were in the forest blocked the sun. Larry shivered, missing the warmth of the sun. He zipped up the zipper of his jacket and kept moving. Some branches that stuck out from the trees reached out and snagged his jacket. He fell quickly to the ground. Larry slowly pulled himself up and slowly turned in a circle. He was completely and totally lost.

2. Take one of your writing samples from a previous activity and rewrite it.

3. Was it hard to know what to change in the previous activities? It's often difficult to see what needs improving in your own work because you are so close to it. That's why critique groups and book doctors can be helpful. But it is possible to revise your own work. Take a fresh look at one of your writing samples and use the chart on page 112 to get started (see chapter 6 for elaborated definitions of some of these concepts).

---

but there are also people known as book doctors who can help. Some of them are reputable former editors and some have questionable backgrounds. Many authors even supplement their incomes by critiquing manuscripts. Of course, both authors and editors have varying degrees of skill. It's best to get references from people you know. If you approach an agent who offers to help you fix your manuscript for a fee, keep walking. Any agent who charges a reading fee is probably not someone you want to work with. The important thing to remember when working with any type of book doctor, be it former editor, author, or agent, is that the story is yours. Just because someone suggests a change doesn't necessarily mean you should do it. Ultimately, it is your story and your final decision.

Mel Boring once told us at a conference that "anyone can be a writer, but not everyone can be a rewriter." Mel knows that rewriting is what turns an ordinary story into something the reader will never forget—a story that really sparkles.

It's not easy. If it were, everyone would be publishing books. Rewriting requires time, patience, and persistence. It's funny that even after reading a story and working on it for months (or in some cases, years), we find things to change. Many authors don't like to read their published works because they still find things they would like to rewrite. Let's face it, a piece of writing can almost always be made better through another revision or two. But there comes a time when you need to push your piece away and prepare to send it out.

So how do you decide when it's time to stop rewriting your work? It's a tough call, but we can usually tell because we're sick of working on it. If that's the case, set your story aside for a few days. If it sounds good when you take it out again, chances are it's ready for the next step in the writing process.

Editing

The next step is editing. This is the stage during which you concentrate on enforcing all those rules your ninth-grade English teacher made you memorize. Hopefully, you learned all that you need for this important stage in your high-school English classes, but Debbie is still amazed by the student in her university-level writing class who asked, "Do I need to know correct grammar to write a children's book?" Of course you do! If you feel uncertain about your grammar and punctuation skills, head to a nearby college for a refresher course. You might just find other writers in the same boat. Another possibility is to dig out that old English textbook and bone up. Libraries and bookstores are good sources for books on correct usage, and it never hurts to have a few references on your desk to help with style and usage questions. Several good hand-

TRY IT YOURSELF: EDITING

1. Choose a sample of your own writing, and edit it using the checklist on the following page. Get out your red pencil and pretend you are a high-school English teacher. Read your own work as if one of your students wrote it. Correct it as you go.
2. Now, give a clean copy of the same writing sample to a real English teacher and ask her to edit it for you. (Make sure it is a short one-page sample because teachers are very busy people.) Now compare your editing with the English teacher's. How did you do? If the teacher found many more mistakes than you did, perhaps it is time to take a grammar class.

EDITING CHECKLIST ✔

Do I have quotation marks where they are needed?

Do I have a noun and a verb in every sentence?

Do I limit my use of exclamation points?

Do I use question marks at the end of every question?

Have I used spell check?

Do I have paragraphs that are too long?

Have I used grammar check?

Do I limit my use of slang? Will my words stand the test of time?

books include *The Elements of Style* by William Strunk Jr. and E.B. White, *The New Oxford Guide to Writing* by Thomas S. Kane, and *The Chicago Manual of Style* by the University of Chicago Press.

Publishing

The final step of the writing process is sometimes the most difficult, but it can also be the most fun. After all, this is the purpose of putting words in print in the first place. Publishing is our ultimate goal. It completes the communication between you and your audience. When your story has been rewritten, edited, and printed, how do you publish it? And what does publishing really mean anyway?

To publish simply means to go public with what you've written. It's the final step that sends your written words to your audience. Most writers hope to be widely published in a book or magazine. There's something very romantic about the idea that people in Utah could be reading the story you wrote from your spare bedroom in Kentucky! If you desire to be widely published, you will need to prepare your stories in proper manuscript format (see chapter 9). You'll also need to find publishers who might be interested in your story. An indispensable source that covers the nuts

TRY IT YOURSELF: PUBLISHING

1. Go to the library or bookstore and browse through the *Children's Writer's and Illustrator's Market*. Select a few publishers that might be interested in some of your story ideas.
2. Visit a friendly classroom. Ask the teacher if you could publish one of your pieces by reading to a group of children.
3. Write a memoir. Publish it by mailing it to family members or reading it at a family gathering.

---

and bolts of writing query letters and finding the right publisher for your work is the *Children's Writer's and Illustrator's Market*, edited by Alice Pope. Another helpful book is *The Writer's Book of Checklists* by Scott Edelstein.

But keep in mind that there are other ways to publish. Some people attend writing groups for the sole purpose of publishing their work in the form of a public reading. They find the warm and supportive environment a risk-free way of sending out their words for others to appreciate.

Another way to publish is by participating in readings at coffee shops, bookstores, literacy centers, and libraries. Performing your work in front of an audience gives you immediate feedback about how your writing is being received.

Self-publishing is another option. Kay Johnson found self-publishing the perfect way to publish her book, *Tales Twice Told: Reflections of a Kentucky Original As Told to Kay Johnson by Her Father Clifton Powell Johnson*. She transcribed her father's stories, editing for the written page, but being careful to maintain his voice. She intended the book as a keepsake for her family.

Tales Twice Told turned into an actual piece of art because Kay bound the twenty-five copies for family members herself. It was such a big hit that she has been asked to speak for the Kiwanis Club, and a small press has showed interest in publishing it as a regional piece.

You don't have to be a bookbinder to self-publish. Vintage or vanity presses are private businesses that will publish your work for a fee. It is often expensive, but many people find it worth the expense if they are writing pieces intended for a small audience. However, self-publishing is usually not a way to make money. If a publisher asks for a fee and you are not making a family keepsake, think twice.

Our Writing Process

True, we've described the writing process as five distinct steps, but writing isn't really that tidy. In fact, it can get rather messy with one step of the process running into another. The truth is, the process isn't sequential at all. It's recursive, with each step doubling back and weaving throughout the process. We call our process "hot-potato" writing. The following describes how we make the writing process work for us.

We start by researching our topic for ideas. After we have enough information, we brainstorm possible story lines. We use many of the strategies described so far. Then we work out a basic plot outline. Our outlines include just a few sentences that tell what could happen in each chapter (more about outlines in chapter 7). As we jot down what might happen in the plot, we often find that we need to do more thinking or research, so back to the Internet or library we go. Sometimes one of us writes an outline draft and sends it to the other writer. Other times one will do a partial outline and the other completes it. Either way, something that one of us wrote usually sparks an idea for the other writer, and the outline is revised and edited to reflect the new ideas.

Once we have the outline, we take turns writing chapters. That's when we start calling it "hot potato." Just like with the game, it's important for neither one of us to drop the "potato" by letting it sit on our desk too long. One of us will write a few chapters based on our outline, then "hot potato" it to the other writer using E-mail. Do you think those chapters are perfect? Of course not! The next writer reads over the chapters written by the first writer. Again, something might trigger more ideas, or maybe the second writer sees the plot progressing differently so she revises the chapters. Of course, if she sees spelling, grammar, or usage errors, she'll edit those, too. Then, using the outline as a guide, she'll write the next few chapters before "hot potato-ing" back to the first writer. And are those chapters perfect? You guessed it! The first

TRY IT YOURSELF: OUR WRITING PROCESS

1. Try writing the hot-potato way. Find a writing partner. Together, brainstorm a story or article idea. Then take turns passing it back and forth. Let the sparks fly!

writer circles back through all the stages of the writing process as she reads the new chapters, is sparked by additional ideas, revises, and edits before writing more.

By the time we've finished the book, we've both worked on all parts of the story. Sometimes we can't even remember who wrote which chapters because they've gone through such a metamorphosis!

Summary

You can't ignite your writing engine and drive off into the sunset unless you have all the necessary parts of the writing machine. Thinking about the fundamental elements of writing will help you collect the parts needed to get your piece revved up and ready to take off in high gear. In this chapter we discussed the writing process and learned how involved it can be.

Now that you have reviewed all the basic components of writing, you're ready to look at strategies that will help you start developing those ideas into full-fledged writing pieces.

SCULPTING YOUR IDEAS

So far we've tried a variety of strategies to help spark ideas. We've spent time considering what is needed to develop those ideas into a story. But what about the nuts and bolts of writing? How do you really get those sparks to flare into full-fledged fiery pieces? Maybe your writing has been like trying to start a wet match. The sparks are there, but they just keep sputtering out. Or maybe you realize your piece is turning more into a treatment; a summary of the idea because you're just not sure how to shape your basic idea into the kind of piece you envisioned.

Marcia once went to the Cannon Beach Sand Castle Contest in Cannon Beach, Oregon. Groups of fun-loving beach-goers piled onto the beach. They claimed their plot of sand and went to work.

Some people merely scooped sand with their hands, mounding it up and then shaping it into sharks or mermaids. Others used typical sand castle tools: buckets, plastic cups, spoons. But the more serious sculptors brought boards, rakes, shovels, knives, art spatulas, and diagrams.

The serious builders consisted of teams. Each team member held detailed diagrams of the team's end goal, drawn from every conceivable angle. One team even came with a model built with modeling clay. They started by building tiered wooden towers on the beach, packing each level with heavy garden tools, constantly pounding and adding water until it was as solid as concrete. The frames were carefully removed to reveal squared-off towers of hardened sand that looked like a giant wedding cake. Then, with spatulas and carving knives, each member carved life into his designated blob of sand.

Writing is much like carving sand. You start with a few loose grains—your ideas. You can mound your words on paper—clumping them together, writing without a real plan, using the few writing techniques you already know—until a vision appears. Then you can chip away until you hopefully discover the true beauty buried within. Another way to develop your idea is to equip yourself with fundamental tools that help you sculpt your story into a solid piece as you write. This chapter will help you fan your creative sparks by reviewing fundamental tools that will help you write with confidence. We'll talk about writing techniques that serve as tools to develop your basic ideas. Let's get started carving your story castle.

Point of View

One of the first things you must determine is who will tell your story. Sure, we know that you are the author, but how are you going to relate the events of your story to the readers? Will it be one of the characters? Will it be an objective narrator? The point of view affects how your story develops. There are several different choices of point of view.

First Person

Stories written in first-person point of view are narrated by one of the story's characters as if it is a personal account of the story's events. First-person narration uses the personal pronoun "I." This creates an intimate retelling of the events since the reader is allowed insight into the character's thoughts and feelings. Here's an example:

> Stanley and Judy stood right behind me in the lunch line. I could hear every word they said.
>
> "We'll meet as soon as it gets dark," Judy said. "And don't chicken out."
>
> "I'll be there," Stanley told her.
>
> I knew Stanley and Judy were planning something big for Halloween. "Where are you going?" I asked.
>
> "None of your business, Hubert," Judy said, her nose sticking straight up in the air.
>
> I hated it when she talked to me like that.

Here, we're seeing the story through Hubert's eyes and ears. Notice that we're given insight into Hubert's feelings, but we aren't allowed into the other characters' heads. Using a first-person narrator limits the story to that specific character. It also means that the story events may be slanted toward Hubert's understanding of the events.

When choosing first person as the point of view, remember that this narrator can only report on events in which he or she is involved. In our example, Hubert won't be able to tell us what happens that night if he isn't there. (Unless, of course, he sneaks up on the other characters and witnesses what they do.)

A benefit of first person is that the reader can become close to the main character and care about what happens to him.

Third Person

Third-person stories are narrated using the pronouns "he," "she," and "they." There are several types of third-person points of view.

Third-Person Omniscient

Third-person omniscient provides the reader with a view of everything. The reader is given access to a variety of characters' actions, words, thoughts, and emotions. This can get complicated and makes it difficult for readers to identify with any of the characters. That's why it isn't used often in children's books. Let's see how the earlier scene would look rewritten with a third-person omniscient point of view.

Stanley and Judy stood right behind Hubert in the lunch line. Stanley glanced at Hubert's big ears. He was afraid Hubert would be able to hear. "Shh," he warned Judy. "We don't want anybody to hear."

Judy shrugged. She didn't care if Hubert or anybody else heard her. As far as she was concerned, the president of the United States could listen in.

"We'll meet as soon as it gets dark," Judy said. "And don't chicken out," she added, poking a finger right in Stanley's chest. She knew Stanley wasn't very brave.

"I'll be there," Stanley told her and batted her finger away. He wasn't about to admit that his knees shook just at the thought of what they were planning.

Hubert knew Stanley and Judy were planning something big for Halloween. They were always up to something. "Where are you going?" Hubert asked.

"None of your business, Hubert," Judy said, her nose sticking straight up in the air.

Hubert hated it when she talked to him like that. Of course, Judy talked to everybody like that.

Like the name implies, third-person omniscient not only lets us see what is happening, but it also allows us inside the heads of all the characters. This can be a bit much to keep up with, so think carefully before using it when writing for young readers.

Third-Person Limited Omniscient

In third-person limited omniscient, the reader is only provided insight into one character's thoughts and feelings—that's what makes it limited. This point of view is similar to first person except it uses the third-person pronouns "he," "she," and "they." Here is our scene rewritten with this limited point of view.

Stanley and Judy stood right behind Hubert in the lunch line. Hubert could hear every word they said.

"We'll meet as soon as it gets dark," Judy said. "And don't chicken out."

"I'll be there," Stanley told her.

Hubert knew Stanley and Judy were planning something big for Halloween. They were always up to something. And for once, Hubert wanted to be included. He turned around and faced them. "Where are you going?" he asked.

"None of your business, Hubert," Judy said, her nose sticking straight up in the air.

Hubert hated it when she talked to him like that. Of course, he knew she talked like that to everybody.

Notice that the viewpoint has shifted back to Hubert. Like first person, third-person limited omniscient allows the reader to identify with one character. But the third-person point of view provides a little distance from the actual story events. This is a popular choice for many authors of children's books.

Third-Person Objective

Third-person objective is written like what a camera would see—only reporting what is said and done. Insight to characters' thoughts and feelings is not given. Similar to watching a play on stage, we see the characters move and hear what they say, but we can't get inside

TRY IT YOURSELF: POINT OF VIEW

1. In what viewpoints are some of your favorite books written? Take a few minutes to find out. Try rewriting a book's passage using different viewpoints to see how it would change the mood and meaning of the narration.
2. Practice writing the following scenes from the first person, third-person omniscient, third-person limited omniscient, and third-person objective viewpoints.
   ⋆ A fight between a brother and a sister
   ⋆ A game between two friends where one of them is cheating
   ⋆ A scene in which three kids are lost in a forest

---

anybody's head or heart. Let's see how our scene unfolds when told with a third-person objective viewpoint.

> Stanley and Judy stood right behind Hubert in the lunch line.
> "We'll meet as soon as it gets dark," Judy said. "And don't chicken out."
> "I'll be there," Stanley told her.
> Hubert turned around and faced Stanley and Judy. "Where are you going?" he asked.
> "None of your business, Hubert," Judy said, her nose sticking straight up in the air.

Choice of viewpoint affects how the story's events are related to the reader. Some writers tend to always use one viewpoint, while others find that changing viewpoints allows them to find the appropriate voice for each particular story.

What point of view do you prefer? Choosing a viewpoint will dictate how scenes unfold as you develop your ideas. Before you start your story you'll need to decide which viewpoint you'll use to narrate. But don't worry if you're not absolutely sure. Some writers find that a story would be much stronger written from a different point of view after they've finished drafting. There's always time to revise!

Voice

Voice—it's difficult to pinpoint and hard to define. Voice is an elusive element that just seems to happen when a writer writes. It's intertwined

123

with style. Style and voice both have to do with the way a writer varies sentence structure, the choice of descriptive words, and even the way words are expressed and put together, otherwise known as syntax.

We all have a distinctive voice. When someone you know calls you on the telephone but doesn't identify himself, chances are you can easily recognize who it is by the way he talks, the sound of his voice, and the way he says things. In other words, you recognize your family and friends by their unique voices and styles of speaking.

The same is true in writing. Writers have unique narrative voices and styles. How we choose to write our sentences and organize our words is known as our writing style. The sound of our writing personality that emerges is called our voice.

Some writers have a lighter style. Seemingly without effort, they write using words that are breezy and easy to read. On the other hand, there are writers who have a more heavy-handed approach to writing. They use descriptive words, lengthy narrative passages, and stronger verbs. Their longer, more complex sentences lend a different mood than short, simple sentences that are more to the point.

Developing your personal writing voice shouldn't be that hard. All you need to do is capture the cadences and tone of your speaking voice. Your voice may be consistent no matter what you're writing, but more than likely it will change to reflect the tone of your story or article. Have you ever noticed how your speaking voice changes depending on the situation? The discussion you have with your boss about why you deserve a raise will sound much different than the argument over marbles you had with your best friend when you were nine years old. So it is with your writing. The voice you use for a story about a fairy princess will likely sound different than the article you write about bicycle maintenance.

If you write fiction in first person, your personal writing voice will also be influenced by your character's personality. Since your character is telling the story, you'll want his or her voice to be evident, not yours. Step back and let the character have her unique voice. How is she feeling? Where is she from? When does she live? The first-person narrator's personality will dictate the writing voice for your story.

What style and voice should you use? That certainly depends on you, what you like, and the characters in your story. Perhaps you have a distinctive natural voice that comes out no matter what. Don't worry if you don't hear that natural writing voice. Even without trying, you have your own voice and style. It might not be strong. You might not like it and you may want to improve it, but you do have it. If you are

TRY IT YOURSELF: VOICE

1. Read several of the Newbery Medal books. What voice and style do the authors use? Are they serious? Are they light?

2. It is OK to model after another author's voice as an exercise. (In the end though, you must develop your own way of writing that comes naturally from everything about you.) Read *The Best Christmas Pageant Ever* by Barbara Robinson. Write a paragraph modeling the distinctive voice from that story.

3. Different stories may call for slightly different styles and voices. For instance, a scary story screams for words like "scream." Try writing a paragraph using the scariest voice you can muster. Remember to use words that are dark and foreboding.

4. Look at one of the freewriting activities you wrote in chapter 2.
    ★ Rewrite it the way you would tell it to your best friend.
    ★ Rewrite it in the voice of a playground thug.
    ★ Rewrite it like the teacher's pet would tell it.
    ★ Rewrite it in the voice of Suzy-who-wears-frilly-dresses.

5. Take an acting class to help you "get into character" and use a variety of voices and styles.

---

not happy with your style and voice, soak in other voices. Read lots of literature that appeals to you. Without trying, you will find that your voice and style will subtly change to reflect the stories you have read.

Word Choice (or the Art of Being Specific)

When writing for children, words are at a premium. Kids will not read through pages and pages of imprecise wording. Editors are definitely not interested in buying long-winded stories. Writers need to use their words effectively, making every one count.

The two basic parts of sentences are nouns and verbs. Nouns identify the subject—who or what the sentence is about. Verbs identify the action—what the subject did or is doing. Since they are the basic constructs of your writing, consider how you can use them to make your writing really stand out.

Verbs and Adverbs

Present Tense vs. Past Tense

There are two major tenses of verbs. Present tense is used when describing things that happen at the same time the story events unfold.

Present tense lends a sense of immediacy to stories because they're written as if they're happening right now. Notice how the following example makes you feel like you're actually witnessing the story as it occurs.

> Jessica tosses the empty bottle out the open window and I hear it shatter on the wet road.
>
> "I don't think you should be driving," I tell her. "Not after drinking."
>
> Jessica laughs so hard she splatters spit on the steering wheel. "There's nothing wrong with me," she says as she turns the key.
>
> I want to open the door and get out, but the car jerks forward. The motor sputters to life too fast. I realize that I'm trapped.

Present tense is great to use when you want to give a sense of urgency to the story. Two excellent examples of novels narrated in present tense are *Here and Then* by George Ella Lyon and *The War in Georgia* by Jerrie Oughton.

It's more common to see children's stories written in past tense, as though the events have already occurred. Past tense distances the reader from the story's events and is told as if the narrator is looking back on what happened. Look how the previous example changes when told in past tense.

> Jessica tossed the empty bottle out the open window and I heard it shatter on the wet road.
>
> "I don't think you should be driving," I told her. "Not after drinking."
>
> Jessica laughed so hard she splattered spit on the steering wheel. "There's nothing wrong with me," she said as she turned the key.
>
> I wanted to open the door and get out, but the car jerked forward. The motor sputtered to life too fast. I realized too late that I was trapped.

Which one did you like best? Whether you choose present or past tense, be consistent. If you begin your story using one tense, stay with that tense throughout.

Active Verbs vs. Passive Verbs

Another thing to consider is whether to make your verbs active or passive. Padding sentences with unnecessary verb phrases or auxiliary (helping) verbs switches the focus of the sentence from the subject to the object of the verb. Sometimes the passive voice can't be avoided, especially if your goal is to emphasize the action or if you're showing a flashback scene, but in general, using active voice is more direct and punchy. Look at the examples below to discover how the active voice promotes more lively writing.

PASSIVE VERBS VS. ACTIVE VERBS

Passive	Active
The car was gunned by Jessica.	Jessica gunned the car.
Werewolves were growling at the cat.	Werewolves growled at the cat.
I had seen her shadow in the hallway.	I saw her shadow in the hallway.

Verb Choice

Specific verb choice is important whether you're writing in past or present tense. Using strong, vivid verbs will make your story come alive. Examine the following sentences to see what we mean.

Mary twirled across the stage, her pink dress swirling around her knees.

Mary stepped and turned quickly three times around on the stage, with her pink dress floating lightly in the air around her.

The first sentence is more effective thanks to the use of precise verbs like "twirled" and "swirling" that accurately describe the action. The first sentence is also shorter and more to the point, which is always a plus when writing for children. As you draft, strive to use the verb that most accurately describes your characters' actions.

Adverbs

Whenever possible, delete adverbs. Adverbs modify the action word, or verb. Adverbs such as "quickly" and "lightly" in the previous example lengthen the sentence and don't accurately show the action. Replacing weak verbs and adverbs with precise verbs strengthens your writing.

Nouns and Adjectives

Noun Choice

Noun choice is important, too. Choosing the word that most precisely names the sentences' subjects helps liven your writing. When writing,

TRY IT YOURSELF: WORD CHOICE

1. Make the following sentences more effective by substituting better words for the existing verbs, adverbs, nouns, and adjectives:
   * ☆ Jason walked slowly past the tall tree.
   * ☆ Lots of rain fell loudly on the top of the big car.
   * ☆ Mary's book dropped quickly onto the living room floor with a loud noise.
2. Find the sentence that does not fit in this paragraph. It will be the one that is written using a different verb tense.

> Easter came early that year. Lilies and tulips surrounded Grandma's old farmhouse. Every year grandma hid fifty eggs for us to find. I see the Easter eggs hidden in the tall grass.

"I see the Easter eggs hidden in the tall grass" is the sentence that needs revising. It is written using present tense while the rest of the paragraph is in past tense. A past-tense version of the sentence could be: I saw the Easter eggs hidden in the tall grass.

---

be specific. Examine the following examples to see how the choice of noun affects the meaning of the paragraph.

> Jesse parked his big car under the flowering tree. He plucked some flowers from the garden before ringing the doorbell. Louise opened the door wearing her pretty dress.

This paragraph is OK. We have two characters and a sense of what might be happening. But look at how the scene changes when we use specific nouns to replace the arbitrary words.

> Jesse parked his Chevy under the crab apple. He plucked some daisies from the garden before ringing the doorbell. Louise opened the door wearing her pretty gingham dress.

To further demonstrate the importance of specific nouns, notice how the selection's mood and meaning changes by merely choosing different nouns.

Jesse parked his Porsche under the magnolia. He stopped to pluck some orchids from the garden before ringing the doorbell. Louise opened the door wearing her pretty taffeta dress.

As you write, use the word that best names the picture in your mind. Accurate nouns help show your readers the scene.

Adjectives

Many writers also rely on adjectives to paint their scenes. But, like adverbs, adjectives at best can only lend support to weak nouns. It's even worse if you use ambiguous modifiers. Let's go back to Jesse and Louise. We made the selection better by using specific nouns, but what about the adjectives? There are a few that we could do without. The words "some" and "pretty" really don't mean anything. Some could be two or it could be three hundred. Our idea of pretty could be entirely different than yours.

Just like adverbs, adjectives need to be deleted or chosen carefully. Instead of relying on weak adjectives to show your scene, use precise nouns. In other words, be specific.

Rhythm

No, we're not talking about dancing here (but if you want to take a break to samba, go right ahead!). Rhythm in writing refers to the sound of the language created by your sentence structures. Just like a song, the cadence of your piece must ebb and flow with a variety of beats that sound natural and engaging to the reader.

Huh? Let's look at it another way.

When you're talking to someone, you vary the structure and lengths of your sentences to make sure the listener stays tuned in to your story. The variety of sentence structures and lengths that you use create rhythm. The same is necessary for writing. Effective sentence rhythm provides greater impact to the meaning of what you're writing. Look at the following to see what we mean.

The dog crossed the street. Bobby watched him. It was a big dog. It looked like a wolf. It wasn't wearing a collar. The dog stopped. It looked straight at Bobby. Bobby wanted to run. His feet felt frozen to the ground.

This example lacks a variety of sentence structures and lengths. Instead, it relies on subject-verb arrangement and short, choppy sentences. If you're writing for a very young audience, this simplistic rhythm might

TRY IT YOURSELF: RHYTHM

1. Analyze three pages from one of your favorite books or articles. How has the author used sentence structure to create a sense of rhythm?
2. Analyze your own writing. Examine one passage. Are all the sentences the same length? Are they structured the same?
3. Read aloud one of your written paragraphs. Try rewriting it by changing the structure and length of at least three sentences.

be appropriate. It allows young readers to use predictable sentence structure to decode the context. But simple sentence structure like this quickly becomes dull to the more sophisticated reader. Also keep in mind that if you're writing books and articles meant to be read aloud, this type of rhythm becomes almost hypnotic and often irritating. Create a more natural and pleasing rhythm by varying the length and structure of your sentences. Look at how our previous scene can be revised.

> Bobby watched the dog cross the street. It was a big dog that looked like a mix between a wolf, a monster, and the devil himself. It wasn't wearing a collar. Bobby doubted if collars were even made that big. Just then, the dog stopped and stared at Bobby. Bobby wanted to run. He tried. But his feet were frozen to the ground.

As you write, consider the following suggestions to help you create effective and pleasing rhythm.

* Vary the length of sentences within any given passage.
* Vary the structure of your sentences.
* Combine simple sentences to make longer complex sentences.
* Use short, punchy sentences for emphasis or suspense.
* Use phrases to break up sentences whose syllables create a sing-songy meter.

Rhythm in Poetry and Verse

Rhythm is even more important if you write verse or poetry. As we said earlier, poetry and verse are difficult to sell because they're so hard to

TRY IT YOURSELF: POETRY

1. Write a simple verse or poem about friendship. Now rewrite your idea in prose. Which way is more effective?
2. If you strongly feel that poetry is important to your story, go to the library and study the following poetic meters.
   * ✶ iamb
   * ✶ trochee
   * ✶ anapest
   * ✶ dactyl
   * ✶ spondee

write well. But kids do love rhyme, and there is a definite demand for well-written rhyming stories. Our advice is don't write verse or poetry unless you really want to. And if you really want to, then know how to do it well.

To write verse and poetry well, consider the rhythm created by your verses and poetry. To define the rhythm, or meter, in poetry and verse, listen to the beat of the syllables in each of your lines. Pay attention to which syllables are emphasized more strongly than others. The rhythmic pattern created by accented and unaccented syllables in lines of poetry is referred to as meter.

The most common flaw in writing poetry and verse is forcing your rhymes and meter. If your meter is too rigid, the verse or poem will quickly lose its freshness and become sing-songy. If you find yourself forcing a rhyme, rethink the entire line in order to maintain natural-sounding language. Don't sacrifice natural language to force your rhyme and meter.

Hooks

Wouldn't it be great if we could just reach up out of the pages of our stories and grab readers with a cane, pull them toward the page, and make them read? Well, you can! A hook is a technique used to reach out and grab readers so they'll want to keep reading.

If you're planning to write longer works of fiction, think about how you can hook readers at the end of each chapter. Chapter hooks provide suspense and make the reader want to turn the page to see what happens. Examine books written for the audience you had in mind. See

TRY IT YOURSELF: HOOKS

1. Go to the library and pull out an armload of novels. Flip through the books and look at the end of every chapter. How does the author hook the reader into reading the next chapter?
2. Examine a stack of picture books. What subtle techniques do authors use to move readers into turning each page? Is it a certain language rhythm? Sentence completion? Suspense?
3. Take a look at poetry written for children. How does the author use rhythm and syntax to lead the reader to the next line?
4. Look at nonfiction articles and books. What techniques do the authors use to hook the reader into reading more?
5. Consider one of the conflicts you brainstormed in chapter 4. What situations could serve as hooks for that conflict? (For example, if you have your kids walking through the forest during a moonless night, a chapter hook could be that their flashlight batteries die.)

---

how long the chapters are in those books, and notice how the author leaves the readers hanging at the end of each chapter. A good place to end a chapter is at the height of tension, when there is a question about what is going to happen next—when the lights go dead, when the kids gasp in surprise, when the dog starts growling. These scene grabbers will make the reader wonder what is going to happen. And that's how you hook them!

"Great," we heard some of you say with a mischievous smile. "I'm not planning to write long pieces of fiction so I don't have to think about hooks."

Wrong!

Hooks are also important in short fiction and even in nonfiction.

If you're contemplating writing a picture book, keep in mind that the writing must draw the reader from one page to the next. A hook on every page helps accomplish this. Picture-book hooks don't have to be drastic. Instead, they are often very subtle. Sometimes, just the phrasing of a sentence will make the reader want to turn the page to bring closure of a sentence or to complete the rhythm of the writing. That works as a hook, too.

Nonfiction also needs hooks that keep readers engaged. Using dramatic statements, questions, and scenes will grab readers and make them continue reading in order to satisfy their curiosity.

A hook is also important on the very first page of your writing. After reading your first page, an editor should know:

★ what type of story you're writing
★ who the main character is
★ what is at stake
★ what the hook of the story is . . . what will make him turn the page.

That's a lot to get across in such a short space. The first-page hook doesn't have to be major, but it needs to be suspenseful enough to encourage the reader to turn the page—and in this case, the reader is your editor. Many editors reject books based solely on a first-page reading!

Hooks engage readers and encourage them to keep turning the pages. As you shape your idea, spend time considering how you can hook your readers.

One-Line Summary

One of the best strategies you can use to develop your pieces is a one-line summary. It's so simple, many writers skip it. But defining your piece using a one- or two-sentence summary can help keep you focused. All you need to do is answer the question: What is my story about? If you can say what your story is about in one (or two) sentences, then you have a real grasp of your focus. If you can't, then you don't have a firm understanding of the story—and if you aren't sure, try to imagine what will happen to young readers trying to make sense of it!

To keep your writing and revising on track, simply write your one-line summary on a sticky note. Put the sticky note on top of each page and as you write ask: How does this page relate to that one-line summary? If

TRY IT YOURSELF: ONE-LINE SUMMARY

1. Practice summarizing the plots of your favorite books by writing one-line summaries.
2. Look back at the conflicts and characters you brainstormed in chapter 4. Practice writing one-line summaries by combining characters and conflicts. Starting with, "This is a story about . . ." will help get you going.

it relates, great. If not, delete or rewrite the page so it supports your one-line summary. When you feel stymied for additional ideas, brainstorm situations or details that support that one-line summary to keep your writing going.

Theme

Brainstorming possible themes for stories is a great way to spark more ideas for your writing. Theme is the underlying focus of your story—the angle, interpretation, or overall picture of what you are trying to say. Theme is the real purpose or reason behind your story. The plot, or story events, work together to show the theme or themes of your fiction. In other words, plot is what happens in your story; theme is what the story is really about. You may be writing a story about a group of kids who learn to work together while battling an evil troll. The plot includes what the kids say and do during their harrowing adventure, but your theme may focus on the value of friendship.

Considering possible themes for your stories can lead you to new and exciting ideas. For example: What other plot events or conflicts could you use to "show" the value of friendship? Check out the chart to see a few of the plot events we brainstormed.

THEME: FRIENDSHIP

Possible Plot Events	★ A boy betrays his best friend's confidence ★ Competition for the lead part in a play jeopardizes a friendship ★ A character learns the value of friendship when helping out a neighborhood senior citizen ★ A girl is forced to choose between friendship and popularity

The catch is that with children's books, it's important to avoid being preachy. You may remember a few of those books from when you were young, but didactic writing is not in demand today. Whatever theme or message you have planned for your story, it must be subtle and naturally develop from the character's actions and the story's events. Readers must discover your theme for themselves without it being forced upon them.

"Oh my gosh!" you may be screaming. "I don't have a theme planned for my story idea!" Don't worry. The good news is that you don't have to plan a theme from the beginning. Your theme may emerge later in your writing. The fact is, if you tell a good story, theme is there.

TRY IT YOURSELF: THEME

Complete the following chart. Brainstorm possible one-line summaries that support the listed themes. The first one is done to get you started.

Kid Themes	One-Line Story Summaries
Betrayal	What happens when your best friend tells all your secrets to the school gossip?
Power/Empowerment	_____
Trust	_____
Differences/Individualism	_____
Competition	_____
Friendship	_____
Fear	_____
Bravery/Heroism	_____
Conflict	_____
Sacrifice	_____
Loss	_____
Change	_____
Honor	_____

Dialogue

Dialogue in children's books is simply a conversation between characters. Dialogue is essential and expected in nearly all forms of children's writing, especially fiction of any length.

Use of conversation helps move the plot and define your characters. Much can be learned just by what characters say to each other as they struggle with the story's conflict. You can easily "show" characters' weaknesses, strengths, and personalities through what they say and how they say it.

Dialogue promotes readability. A page filled with no dialogue is pretty overwhelming to a young reader. The use of dialogue opens up a page and makes it more reader-friendly by creating white space. Even older readers can be put off by dense narration filling a page. Think about it. Have you ever opened a book you thought about reading but ended up putting it back on the shelf when you discovered every page was nothing but dense narration? Dialogue breaks up the narration, making the story more readable.

As you prepare to write, keep the following in mind about the words your characters say, and how they say it.

Writing Effective Dialogue

★ **Characterize.** Provide each character with a different and distinct personality. Make sure their unique personalities are evident by their speech. One way to check this is to have someone read your story aloud to you without identifying who is speaking. If you can't tell who says what, try revising the dialogue to make the personalities more obvious.

★ **Be real.** Make sure your characters talk the way kids really talk. Again, read your dialogue out loud. If it doesn't ring true, revise it.

★ **. . . But not too real.** Dialogue must actually be better than real-life speech. During our everyday conversations we use many fillers like "um" and "you know" and "It's like. . . ." Using speech fillers in your written dialogue only delays your story and distracts readers.

★ **Make every word count.** Real-life conversations also include pleasantries and tangential comments. In fiction it's better to skip all the pleasantries and get right to the meat of the conversation. If the dialogue doesn't have a specific purpose for moving and supporting your plot, delete it.

★ **Keep it short.** Most children don't speak in long paragraphs, and neither should your fictional kids. Break up big chunks of dialogue with interaction and action.

★ **Avoid slang.** Slang can be really groovy. It's, like, the cat's meow. Slang is rad; it's hip; it's the bee's knees. But it can obviously date you and your story, because slang changes with every generation. Better to avoid slang so your story can be enjoyed for years.

★ **Punctuate.** Use correct punctuation and paragraph indentation to facilitate readability. Remember: Quotation marks surround the spoken words, and a new paragraph begins each time a different character speaks. Here is an example:

"I don't need any help," Santa told his sister.

Santa's sister frowned. "But I can do lots of things like making toys and reading letters from the girls and boys," she said.

★ **Tag.** Identify who is speaking with a tag to help reduce reader confusion. There's no need to get overly creative with your tags. Using too many different tags like "she grumbled" and "he responded" is unnatural and distracting. "Said" is an invisible word while "hissed," "screamed," and "shouted" stand out. Most often a writer wants the tags to be invisible. Simply adding "he said" or "she said" is best.

TRY IT YOURSELF: DIALOGUE

1. Choose two characters you developed in chapter 4 and let them have a conversation. Take this written dialogue and read it out loud with a friend as if in a play. Does your dialogue sound natural? Are you able to tell who is speaking? If not, try changing the dialogue of at least one of the characters to indicate a different personality.
2. Listen to children talking. It's important for your writing to sound as natural as those kids' real-life dialogue.
3. Examine dialogue in children's books and stories. How do those authors make dialogue sound real?

Show, Don't Tell

If you've read much about writing, you've probably heard the mantra, "Show, don't tell." It seems to be a writer's number-one rule. But what does it really mean?

Simply put, it means that you want to "show" your story's events unfolding rather then "tell" what's happening with description and explanation. For example, we could *tell* you:

Randy was mad.

Or we could *show* you using dialogue and action:

Randy stomped into the room and threw his books across the room. "I hate my teacher," he screamed.

The second example uses dialogue and action to show what mad is—without ever actually saying the word "mad." Action and dialogue bring "mad" to life. As you shape your ideas into stories, look for places where the characters can be given free rein to "show" what's happening.

Figurative Language

Another way to show your scene is through figurative language. Figurative language refers to the techniques you employ to help readers "see" a picture in their minds. Two common techniques are metaphors and similes.

Metaphors and similes assist readers in visualizing what you have in your mind by drawing comparisons to seemingly unrelated objects or concepts.

TRY IT YOURSELF: FIGURATIVE LANGUAGE

1. Rewrite the following telling statements in order to show. Remember to show dialogue and action without telling.
   * ★ Molly was scared.
   * ★ My parents were fighting.
   * ★ The teacher was mad.
   * ★ His dog was playful.
   * ★ She was beautiful.
2. Show the following using metaphors and/or similes.
   * ★ Blue sky
   * ★ Loud voice
   * ★ Soft fur
   * ★ Fast runner
   * ★ Mean teacher

Metaphor

A metaphor is an implied comparison of two unrelated objects or concepts. An example would be:

The moon was a silver dollar in the night sky.

Simile

A simile is an indirect comparison of two unrelated objects using the word "as" or "like." Here is a simile:

The moon was like a silver dollar in the night sky.

As you write, use metaphors and similes to help readers make connections and see relationships. But beware of trite and clichéd figures of speech that might date your writing instead of making it fresh and alive.

Summary

Like a sand castle, every story needs a proper foundation. In the case of your story, you need to determine the point of view, your voice, and your tense. In sculpting your castle of a story, be careful of word choices. Use active verbs and specific nouns. Whether writing poetry or prose, vary sentences in structure and length to have a pleasant rhythm.

Who will want to read your story? Everyone because you have used enticing hooks to keep readers' eyes fixed to the page. Have hooks at the beginning and end of every chapter.

One essential foundation in nearly all children's books is the use of dialogue. Keep your story castle standing tall for years to come with natural and lively conversation.

Now that you've collected a few writing tools to help you develop your writing ideas, let's take a look in the next chapter at a few organizational tools that will facilitate your writing.

A FIRM FOUNDATION

Using the correct tense and staying in the same point of view throughout your entire story is, of course, important. Your story castle can be a shining example of expertly shaped ideas, but if you get lost in the maze of rooms while writing, you may never even finish. If you are confused with where your story is going, imagine how befuddled your reader will be.

While some authors refuse to use organizational techniques to aid their writing, we think they are the foundation for any successful story castle. In this chapter we focus on ways to organize your ideas to ignite your drafting stage. We'll also help you assess your potential pieces for appropriate genres and audiences and how that might impact the direction of your writing.

Outlines

No, no, no! We're not talking about the kind of outlines that make all good English teachers giggle with delight—Roman numeral, followed by capital letter, followed by numeral, followed by lowercase letter. Outlines like those may actually interfere with the creative process because they're so formal and rigid. Too many rules only stifle the creative urge. After all, how can you expect your muse to feel playful when she's too busy remembering how to make the number eight into a Roman numeral?

If that's the case, why even bother talking about outlines?

It is true that there are restrictions to outlining your writing pieces. But there are also benefits to planning your writing projects using some type of outlining process. The following chart highlights a few of the benefits and restrictions to consider when outlining your work.

OUTLINING	
Benefits of Outlining	**Restrictions of Outlining**
Outlining may benefit your writing when the following occurs.	Outlining may restrict your writing if the following occurs.
1. Your creativity is enhanced because your outline keeps your writing focused—it isn't cluttered by unrelated ideas.	1. Your creativity is inhibited, because you become too focused on the outlining process instead of the writing process.
2. You consider your outline as a direction for your writing, and you feel free to elaborate.	2. Your writing becomes rigid and sparse, because you find yourself limited by what is written on the outline.
3. You use the outline as a general guide but understand that new ideas are welcome—even if they do change your outlined proposal for writing.	3. You are reluctant to explore new ideas that develop naturally during the writing process, because you would need to veer away from the outline.
4. The outline becomes a work-in-progress that grows, develops, and changes along with your writing process.	4. You delay writing, because you can't finish the outlining process. The result: frustration and self-doubt.

Outlining before writing helps organize all the sections or scenes of your entire piece and provides a guide you can use during the writing process. Using outlines is rather like planning a road trip. You know where you want to go—your destination. You look at a map and plan your route, taking note of all the interesting stops you'll make along the way. Knowing this information before you pull out of the driveway reduces stress and allows you to enjoy the scenery as you go.

Like a road trip, planning your pieces with an outline helps you focus on your destination and the necessary turns you'll need to make. You also can make sure you schedule time to take in all the interesting sight-seeing stops along the way. Mapping your piece prior to writing makes the actual drafting process easier and faster, too. Your mind is uncluttered by unanswered questions, and you avoid unnecessary side roads that lead to nowhere and wrong turns that get you hopelessly lost. That's why many writers outline before they write. Outlining helps you collect and organize the necessary details you'll need to elaborate your basic plot or idea, and it makes drafting easier.

On the other hand, if you plan your trip right down to the exact time of arrival, chances are you'll be so focused on your destination you'll end up zooming by all those unexpected scenic overlooks and quaint antique junk shops. You'll also miss hidden side roads that lead to waterfalls and go-cart parks. And what if you're not really sure of your destination? Does that mean you should just spend the week on the couch watching television instead of venturing out?

Many writers believe writing is a discovery process. They don't want to know where they're going. They just want to get in the car and drive without having the restrictions of a plan that might inhibit the natural discovery of ideas.

Whether or not you decide to outline is entirely up to you. You might try developing an outline, or at least part of one. Then, try another project without any plan at all. See what works the best for you.

There are many ways to construct your writing plans, or outlines. Formal outlines that you learned in school are just one way. They use rigid rules dictating where to place your main ideas and supporting details. If that works for you, great. If not, take a look at some of the other book planners provided in this chapter.

Listing

The easiest way to organize your writing project is to list the topics or chapters you plan to include in your piece. This provides a sequential list of subtopics to guide your writing. Let's use the brainstorming about ants that we did in chapter 2 as an example. A simple outline might look like the following.

Ants
1. Ant behavior
2. Ant physiology
3. Ant bites
4. Ant architects

This provides a very simple outline, but it doesn't include details about the subtopics.

Subtopic

You may want a little more direction than what is provided in a simple list. A subtopic chart like the one we used in chapter 2 can help by encouraging you to group your details into appropriate subtopic headings.

SUBTOPIC OUTLINE

Title: *Busy As Ants*

One-line summary: Information article about ants.

Subtopic 1: Ant Behavior	Subtopic 2: Ant Physiology	Subtopic 3: Ant Bites	Subtopic 4: Ant Architects
★ Marching	★ Relative strength	★ Biting ants	★ Tunneling systems
★ Carrying big loads	★ Colors	★ Harmless ants	★ Job divisions and
★ Eating	★ Bodies	★ Fire ants	specialization
★ Social structure	★ Antennae	★ Bite treatment	★ Ant mounds/hills
★ Job divisions/ Job	★ Body	★ Avoiding bites	★ How long it takes to
specialization	★ Functions	★ Poisonous ants	build tunnels/hills
★ Perseverance	★ Sizes	★ Ants in your pants	★ Cooperation during
★ Cooperation	★ Legs		constructions
★ Motivation	★ Diseases		★ Soil and tunnels
			★ How long a tunnel lasts
			★ How tunnels and hills survive rain and wind

This type of outline is easy to use. Label columns with the categories, subtopics, or chapters you plan to cover. Once you determine the categories, you can organize your ideas and research into clusters for possible writing. Then, when you're ready to draft, just write about what's in the columns.

Synopses of Sections

Maybe you're more like us. We use lists to help us start organizing our ideas, but then we like to include more of a synopsis for each chapter or section. Sometimes we even include bits of dialogue and descriptions that we already know we want to use. If that's the case, try outlining your story idea into chapter or section synopses like the one on page 145 that's based on our web from chapter 2.

Briefly summarizing each chapter or article subtopic in your writing piece is an effective outlining strategy to help keep your writing on track.

Story Elements

In chapter 4 we reviewed the elements of fiction and nonfiction writing. Outlining with these elements in mind is an effective guide for

Title: *The Bride of Frankenstein Doesn't Bake Cookies*

Chapter/ Section	One-line summary: The kids think the new cookie baker is the bride of Frankenstein.
1	The cookies at the ice-skating rink are tiny and dry. Eddie thinks that's why Frank, their monster hockey coach, is so sad. Liza isn't so sure. She thinks it's because Frank is lonely. After all, the original Frankenstein monster didn't have any friends. Maybe Frank doesn't either. Dr. Victor, the scientist from the Shelley Museum, walks in and sees Frank crying at the cookie counter.
2	On the way home, Howie warns his friends that a sad monster could be dangerous. They have to hurry home before a storm hits Bailey City. Before they go inside, Howie is sure he sees a huge bolt of lightning strike the Shelley Museum.
3	There's somebody new behind the snack counter at the ice-skating rink, and she's serving up monster cookies. Dr. Victor introduces her as his niece, Electra. Howie is sure she's a monster created as a friend for Frank. Eddie doesn't care. He likes the cookies.
4	Melody says they should be careful of the cookies. She thinks Electra used Formula Big to create monster cookies. Formula Big is what they think Dr. Victor used to make Frank. They remember seeing Frank using the same formula to grow giant petunias. If they eat the cookies, they may all turn into monsters.
5	The kids notice that Electra is so busy selling her new cookies that she doesn't have time to notice Frank. Frank is upset. He tries to get Electra's attention, but Electra doesn't notice.
6	Frank is desperate to get Electra's attention. He shows off on the ice. When he does, he falls. Everybody laughs. Even Electra.
7	Frank leaves the rink. Howie warns his friends that they are in danger. The original Frankenstein monster was so upset when people didn't like him he destroyed the castle. What if Frank destroys Bailey City? They have to do something. Are they too late?

your writing. Let's compare it to our road trip we talked about earlier. Before you set out on a vacation you take time to pack all the things you're going to need: shorts, swimsuit, sunscreen, a few good books. You might even make a list and then check off each item as you pack it.

Using charts that focus on the elements of writing is a similar process. They include prompts to help you remember to think through each of the necessary elements to include for your story or article.

Thinking through the elements of fiction will ensure that you're packing all the necessary items you'll need for your story. Take a look at the following example (on page 146) to see what we mean.

STORY ELEMENTS

Title: *Redwall* by Brian Jacques

One-line summary: Adventure story about a battle between peaceful mice and warrior rats.

Character Who is this story about?	Matthias, a peaceful mouse reared by the gentle mice of Redwall Abbey.
Setting Where and when does this story happen?	The Summer of the Late Rose in a place called Mossflower in Redwall Abbey.
Conflict What problem must the character solve?	Cluny the Scourge tries to take over Redwall Abbey, Matthias's home.
Climax What crisis forces the character to either succeed or fail?	Cluny tries to take over the Abbey.
Resolution How has the character changed or grown?	Matthias has changed from a clumsy boy to the hero of Redwall Abbey.
Plot What happens in this story? Why and how does it happen?	Matthias uses every resource to outwit Cluny, culminating in a battle and Cluny's death.

Plot Events

Another outline plan for fiction writing involves jotting down your major story events and looking at how they result in complicating your plot. The goal of this plan is to show how the conflict builds in intensity as characters struggle with their conflict as in the example on page 100. In this outline, look at the major events in your story, determine how your main character will react to that event, and see what happens as a result of your character's actions. The cause-and-effect relationships build in intensity to strengthen your original conflict and create suspense for your plot.

This type of outline helps you plan the rising action that's necessary in works of fiction. It also keeps you focused on your main idea so you don't wander too far off the main road.

Fiction-Book Planners

All the outline planners we've looked at so far provide a brief direction for your writing. But you might be the type of writer who prefers a more in-depth plan and wants to map out as much of your fiction story as

Title: *Frankenstein Doesn't Plant Petunias*

Plot: One-line summary telling what the book is about	Kids believe Frankenstein is living at a local museum.
Theme: Word or phrase that tells the deeper, worldly truth that the book is really about	"Don't judge a book by its cover."
Main character(s) and brief personality description	Melody—sensible, adventurous, brave
	Howie—intellectual, serious
	Liza—worrier, scared, believer
	Eddie—impulsive, troublemaker, nonbeliever
Antagonist: A brief personality description of the adversary of the main character	Frank—doesn't speak, has scars, loves petunias, afraid of fire
	Dr. Victor—secretive, cracks knuckles
Conflict: What is at stake?	Surviving a monster
Complications that thicken the plot	1. Abandoned by bus
	2. Storm
	3. Frank has a gun
	4. Dead-end hallway
	5. Find locked refrigerator
	6. Dr. Victor catches kids in secret laboratory
	7. Power outage
	8. Crashing sound
	9. Mrs. Jeepers gets hurt
	10. Storm damages greenhouse
Setting of place and time	Shelley Science Museum outside of fictional town of Bailey City: Now.
Climax: Briefly describe the turning point or moment of no return.	Frank has the kids trapped in a greenhouse during a terrible storm.
Conclusion: Where will the characters be at the end? What has changed?	Kids leave Shelley Museum with different opinion of Frank.

possible. If that's the case, consider using a more comprehensive fiction-book planner. The examples of book planners on page 147 and 148 consider most of the writing tools we covered in the previous chapter as well as chapter-by-chapter synopses.

Whew! These outlines look like work. Well, maybe they are. But in the same way planning a car trip makes your vacation more enjoyable, taking a few days to think through your story using an outline may make the writing easier. (The key word in that sentence is *may*!)

As in any formal process, adhering too strictly to one of these outline plans could actually inhibit your creativity—exactly like those outlines your ninth-grade teachers made you do. If you get too caught up concentrating on the process of outlining and planning, you could end up stifling

FICTION-BOOK PLANNER: CHAPTER SYNOPSES

Title: *Frankenstein Doesn't Plant Petunias*

Main Events	How Events Relate to the Theme
1. Kids are on bus, headed for a museum field trip.	Talk about a previous electrical storm Eddie prejudges field trip
2. Describe the Shelley Museum. Bus leaves as kids enter. Liza recognizes the building from something.	Negative comments about building's appearance Lightning
3. Meet Frank, who looks like Frankenstein. Meet Dr. Victor, the museum curator. Liza summarizes the famous Frankenstein story.	Jump to conclusions about Frank and what they think is a gun in his pocket Lightning, wind
4. Kids play at bubble exhibit until Melody and Liza go in search of a bathroom. The girls get lost. They hear a crash.	Melody and Liza assume Frank is chasing them to hurt them. Lightning
5. They find a greenhouse filled with petunias. Frank is spraying the plants with a water gun. Frank comes after the girls. They run into Howie and Eddie as they flee. They all end up in a secret science laboratory. Kids investigate/question Dr. Victor's secret science laboratory. The lights go dead.	Draw conclusions about what they find in the laboratory Lightning, thunder
6. A power outage. How will they find their way back? Dr. Victor finds them. Dr. Victor lights candles so kids may continue exploring exhibits. Frank sees candles and is afraid of the flames. He runs from the room. They hear a crash. Their teacher leaves them to investigate the noise. The kids follow her.	They jump to conclusions about Dr. Victor and his experiments. Lightning, hail
7. They end up back in the greenhouse. The storm has knocked down a wall. Their teacher is hurt. Frank towers over them, but as the wind blows he struggles to save the plants.	The kids assume Frank is a monster and is trying to destroy the museum. The kids believe Frank is going to hurt their teacher.
8. Frank saves Liza and their teacher when the roof collapses. Liza then helps Frank save his petunias. Dr. Victor rushes in. As he helps gather the plants, he notices the huge blooms. He finds a bottle labeled FORMULA BIG. Dr. Victor is very upset.	See that Frank was only trying to save his flowers. Rain slows to drizzle, sun comes out.
9. The class leaves the museum. Frank gives each kid a potted petunia. All the petunias are huge.	The kids realize it doesn't matter what Frank looks like; he can still be a good friend. Wet steps, sunshine

TRY IT YOURSELF

1. Go to the library and find an interesting article, story, or book. Use one of the suggestions from this section to outline your library selection to discover its internal structure. Blank charts are provided in Appendix G for your use.
2. Which outlining suggestion best matches your personality and writing style? Pick one to try. Use one of the story ideas you brainstormed in chapter 4 to start an outline. Don't spend too much time on it. Just get the feel of what it might take to use outlining in your writing.

the free-flow of ideas that naturally occurs as you draft. So don't let the outlining be your excuse for not actually writing.

Marcia likes using a combination of these planners, but she doesn't worry about having one or all filled out before writing. She jots down what she knows and spends time brainstorming or researching additional information as much as possible. Then she writes. As she discovers more through drafting, she continues to fill in the missing pieces on her planners. After finishing the drafting process, she uses her planners, or outlines, to help find gaps in her story. These gaps become areas for possible revising.

Assessing Audience and Appropriate Genres

Should you write an article or concentrate on turning your idea into a young-adult novel? Is your idea better suited as a mystery or a picture book? Fairy tale or humorous fiction? Do you really need to know this before you start writing?

What makes a good picture book will not necessarily make a good story for fourth graders. The same idea may not be appropriate for all levels. A book about premarital sex would not work as a picture book, and a fourth grader would never come near a book about potty training. But if you take that same baby character and write a book about a super baby, then that same fourth grader may find it worthwhile.

Obviously, potty training is not for older kids and premarital sex is not for preschoolers, but some subjects are harder to judge. Is a book about dogs for third graders, first graders, or middle-school students? Speaking generally, a middle-school student may not be interested, but it certainly depends on how the idea is treated in the story. The classics *Where the Red Fern Grows* and *Shiloh* are intended for fourth through sixth graders. Both of them are well-loved dog stories. The stories are not told through the dog's eyes. Is that the key to writing a dog story for older readers? Not necessarily. The popular Hank the Cowdog series by John R. Erickson is told through a dog's eyes, as are James Howe's Howliday Inn books. The key is that all are well-written stories with strong main characters who we love. None of them are didactic and none talk down to the reader.

So will any age child read a dog story? Probably. What about a cat story? Probably. Any animal? Probably. The key in many instances is not the subject but how the author takes that subject and molds it to the correct level. But exactly how do you do that?

You need to become familiar with the reading level of kids. *Children's Writer's Word Book* by Alijandra Mogilner suggests language appropriate for different ages of children. Another way to learn reading levels is to study the chart of selected books from different genres in chapter 1 (pages 23–25). The books in that chart act as a good measuring stick of what works with different age groups.

In addition, you need to be familiar with what kids do at certain ages. A book about snowboarding would probably not be a hit with a kindergartner, unless it was about a dog having an adventure on a snowboard to save Christmas. Older readers might love the details and tips included in a nonfiction article about snowboarding. Being around children and immersing yourself in their world will help you determine what age level your idea is perfect for. Until you feel more confident, don't hesitate to find articles and books similar to what you imagine your finished piece looking like to help guide your writing.

Another way to ascertain if an idea is right for a certain age is to go to the source. Ask a child who is the age you are targeting about your idea. What is his reaction? But don't stop there. Ask several more kids. If they seem to think it's a good idea, write a few pages and read it to them. Do they roll their eyes and look for the nearest exit? Or do they want you to read more?

In short, some ideas may not work for all genres. But many ideas can be adapted to fit different age groups. If you're writing fiction, keep in mind that the characters need to be the same age or even a few years older than your intended audience. Kids don't mind reading about characters who are like them or older and more sophisticated characters. They don't usually like reading about characters younger than they are.

If you are determined to write for a particular age or genre, keep

TRY IT YOURSELF

Look at our Selection of Children's Literature chart in chapter 1 on pages 23–25. Examine each book for the story idea and what age the reader will be. Make your own chart below to help you get a handle on appropriate topics.

Title	Age	Idea

that focus in mind as you write. It will impact your word choice, syntax, and content. But remember, it isn't necessary to restrict your writing. It's better to write the best story or article you can. If you start out writing a nonfiction article about the African veldt, and you end up writing a young-adult novel about apartheid, don't worry. All that means is that your marketing strategies will need to be revised.

Summary

To sculpt your ideas into effective writing pieces, you must equip yourself with specific tools. This chapter has provided you with the nuts and bolts necessary to help you effectively organize the ideas you've been brainstorming throughout this book.

The planners included in this chapter will help ignite your drafting stage by providing a direction as you work to shape your ideas. If you don't spend time mapping them out before you take off, you could end up wandering the back roads and getting lost. Finally, assessing your potential pieces for appropriate genres and audiences will impact the direction of your writing.

Now let's find out what happens when your sparks start to sputter to life.

CHAPTER 8

WHEN YOUR BATTERY DIES

Writing Through Writer's Block

What do you do when your idea spark starts to sputter to life? It's time to put your engine in gear and roll! But what happens if that idea starts to fizzle and die? So far we've identified markets and studied the basic elements of writing. So we should be ready—but maybe it's just not enough.

Some folks find that first blank page so intimidating they refuse to write. Or they can't think of how to start that first sentence so they don't get past it. They have classic writer's block. It's a horrible disease that no doctor can cure.

But we can. We can cure writer's block because we don't believe there is such a thing. We believe a person can always write. You may not always write well; in fact, your writing may stink at times. But we've found that sometimes you have to write crap to get through to all the glorious words underneath. It's like digging for gold. You have to cut through a lot of worthless rock to find the nuggets.

Persistence is the key to cutting through that bad writing. You're not alone; everyone writes bad stuff. Tell yourself it's OK and get on with it. If you work long enough and hard enough you will get to the good stuff. In this chapter, we'll discuss the following strategies that will keep your words flowing while you develop your ideas in case your writing fizzles.

Strategies to keep the words flowing:

Research to Enrich Ideas
Write Out of Sequence
Give Yourself Permission to Fail
Recognize Your Distractions and Excuses
Set Page or Word Quotas
Enroll in a Writing Class or Workshop
Collaborate With a Friend
Join a Writers Group
Read a Great Book
Review the Previous Day's Work
Write a Letter to Your Audience
Keep an Open Mind
Set Attainable Goals

Research to Enrich Ideas

Every book we write requires research. We may research the legend behind a folkloric character, a time period, or a historical figure's life. Researching adds depth to your piece, even if it's pure fiction. Digging into your topic can provide ideas and angles you may not have considered.

You can begin your research in many ways.

* **Internet:** The Internet is the newest tool in the research field. It can be extremely valuable in locating hard-to-find information. Keep in mind that anyone can have a Web site. We have one: http://www.baileykids.com. You can have one, too, just by typing in a few things and paying a few fees. The point is that everything on the Internet cannot be taken as gospel truth, especially if it comes from a private Web site. The Internet can be fun to browse when you have all the time in the world, but if your time is limited, you may want to limit your searches.

* **Library:** We love the library. It is a writer's first love; a place to browse and dream. (You can dream about having hundreds of books with your name on them to fill those shelves!) It's also a place to research. A good librarian's friendship is not to be overlooked as a basic key in library research. A good research librarian is like a dog with a bone. Give him a question to find out about,

TRY IT YOURSELF: RESEARCH

1. Research an interesting idea on the Internet. Don't forget to take notes and write down where you got the information.
2. Go to the library and talk to your librarian. Establish a relationship by telling him you are a writer for children. If you're not familiar with the library, ask for a tour. While you're at it, find out what kind of book the librarian would like to see published.
3. While you're at the library, ask a librarian to show you the periodic catalog. Also take a look at the list of current magazine holdings. Make a note of any that might be valuable to you. Browse through the stacks if possible.
4. Visit local museums. It's helpful if you have an assignment in mind. Perhaps you are looking for the type of shoes they wore in 1848 or the type of clothing a girl would wear in the early 1900s. If you don't have an assignment, just go and enjoy yourself. If you find something interesting, a child might be interested in it as well.

and nothing will do until he finds the answer.

⋆ **Magazines:** Don't forget about current events—and even not-so-current events. Old magazines can be treasure troves for wonderful tidbits to enhance your stories. Ask your librarian how to use their online periodic catalog for current articles, but don't forget to take a few moments to browse through dusty old volumes. Sometimes the best ideas occur by accident.

⋆ **Museums:** Debbie's son begged to go to the Field Museum in Chicago to see the mummy exhibit. Sure, she thought, it will be educational. She didn't realize that it also would be an inspiration for a book, *Mummies Don't Coach Softball*. If you are fortunate enough to live close to a large museum, don't rule it out as a wonderful place to develop ideas. If you live in a small town, don't despair. Even the smallest towns may have a historical society or some tiny museum in a nearby public library. Visit it with an open mind. Don't forget to talk to the curators. They may have a wealth of interesting old stories about people in your town—people who'd be wonderful to write about. If the curators know you are a writer, they might suggest people to write about. In fact, they may be able to let you know about an entire museum dedicated to your subject.

★ **Interviews and letters:** Don't forget about real people in your research. If you're writing about a historical figure, look for relatives or people who really knew the person you're researching. It will put an entirely new perspective on your writing and bring your character to life.

Write Out of Sequence

There is no golden rule in writing that says you must write the beginning of your piece, then the middle, and finish with the ending. If you have a terrific idea for an ending, don't let it slip by. Starting with the last sentence might even be a plus, because you know exactly where you want your story to go, and you can build everything up to that point. Maybe you can see the scene that will occur in the middle of your story. Don't wait. Write it down! It may never be as good later—if you can even remember it. Computers are wonderful tools that allow you to put the pieces of your story together like a jigsaw puzzle.

If you feel like your idea is fizzling, skip ahead and write out of sequence. Write those scenes, lines, and dialogue snippets when you think of them.

Give Yourself Permission to Fail

The main reason people don't succeed is that they are afraid of failing. You can never fail if you don't try; then again, you can never succeed it you don't try. Give yourself permission to fail. Tell yourself it doesn't have to be perfect. It's OK to write the worst story in the history of the world! Remember that if you write a book, you will have done more than all those people who only talk or think or dream about it. Remember also that all writers are a bit scared when they start new projects. Writing is a scary business. You are creating a new world for your

TRY IT YOURSELF: WRITE OUT OF SEQUENCE

1. Select one of your ideas and write a last sentence for an article. Can you build your story up to that last moment?
2. Write a scene that might happen in the middle of your plot for your character.

TRY IT YOURSELF: PERMISSION TO FAIL

1. Sit down and make yourself comfortable. Now, write the worst story you have ever written in your life. Make it horrible.
2. Now that you've written your horrible story, don't you feel refreshed? (And for you cheaters out there who didn't do it, you don't know what you've missed.) Anytime you start feeling down about your writing, give yourself permission to fail. The results might surprise you.

readers, but don't let it overwhelm you. Just try for the best story you can write and go from there.

Recognize Your Distractions and Excuses

I can't write today because I have to do laundry before I end up naked. I can't write today because I have to brush my cat's teeth. I can't write today because after I do the laundry I have to empty the lint from the dryer. I can't write today because my two-year-old is running me ragged.

How many excuses can you list for not writing today? We can come up with a lot. But they are only that—excuses. They aren't legitimate

EXCUSES VS. REALITY

Excuses	Reality
I have to clean the house.	In fifty years, it will not matter if your house was spotless, but someone could still read your book.
I have to cook supper.	Sandwiches are filling.
I only have time to write a little each day.	A little each day adds up. One page a day equals 365 pages at the end of the year.
I can't afford a computer.	Margaret Mitchell wrote *Gone With the Wind* with a typewriter. Besides, many libraries have computers you can use. Perhaps there's even one at work you could use during your breaks.
I have to work and I'm too tired afterwards.	It's a sad but true fact of life—if we want to be writers, we have to go the extra mile and try even when we're exhausted. If you really want to write, then write. You deserve it. Do it for you.
My ideas are dumb.	Everyone has dumb ideas. Sometimes those dumb ideas make great stories. (Those are probably the ones you hear that make you say, "I could have thought of that!")

TRY IT YOURSELF: EXCUSES

Make up your own excuses list using the following blank chart, only instead of a reality section, give yourself simple solutions to your excuses.

EXCUSES VS. SOLUTIONS	
Excuses	Solutions

reasons. If you really want to write, there are no legitimate excuses. We are all busy people. We all have the same amount of time. Some of us have lots of things to do in that time. But you will find a way if you really want to write. If you tend to fall into the trap of being distracted by your excuses, examine the reality of your situation. Take a look at the chart on page 157 to see what the reality is of our excuses.

Perhaps you think you're the busiest person in the world and there's no way you can find an extra minute. We beg to differ. Do you sit in traffic? Do you have five minutes in the evening before you go to bed? Do you get a lunch break? Do you watch TV? Do you go to the bathroom? Writing can be combined with all of those everyday activities. If you really want to write you *can* find the time. It's a mind-set. Instead of saying, "There's no time," look for little snippets of time to jot down thoughts, character sketches, and overheard dialogue. When you start to look for minutes, you will find them.

When looking for minutes, keep in mind that it is possible to say no to some things. Try it occasionally, you might even like the sound of it. "No, I'm not going to make the bed today. I'm going to write." "No, I'm not going to be room mom this year. I have taken another job. I am a freelance writer." "No, I can't go to lunch on Tuesdays, I have some work to do at my desk." Saying no may be the beginning of a rewarding writing career.

Set Page or Word Quotas

"I will not get up from this chair until I write one page!" Sometimes committing to write a page or a specific number of words will get you

TRY IT YOURSELF: QUOTAS

1. Each day for a week, set a goal to write one page a day. Don't worry if the writing is not perfect. It will get better.
2. Each day for a week, set a goal to write twenty minutes a day. Don't worry if the writing is not perfect. It will get better!
3. Which activity did you like better? Did you prefer striving to write a certain number of words or pages, or did committing to a specific amount of time work better? Use your favorite quota for a month until you establish your writing pattern. You may not need it after that, or you may find it so helpful that you will continue it forever.

---

going. Now, maybe that page won't be a great literary work. Maybe the next won't be either. Don't be too hard on yourself. Rome wasn't built in a day, and neither was the greatest author. Allow yourself time to grow, but in order to grow and learn you must write. Write as often as you can. Page or word quotas are a way to start.

Enroll in a Writing Class or Workshop

There is no substitute for a warm body. No, we're not talking about getting amorous. We're talking about meeting fellow authors and discussing the writing craft. Attending classes and workshops devoted to writing can be just the prescription for ailing writing. Networking is a big buzzword nowadays, and it's a wonderful way to establish contacts who will be invaluable in the years to come. There are many good reasons to enroll in a writers class, workshop, or conference.

* Find people to discuss writing concerns. Don't be afraid to discuss issues that trouble you. Other people have the same problems, too.
* Find people to help you learn how to be a better writer.
* Find people who might want to join a weekly or monthly critique group.
* Meet editors who, now that they've met you, might look at something you've sent them. There's no substitute for the personal connection.
* Learn more about the types of books being published.
* Cure the isolation that many writers feel. You are not alone.

TRY IT YOURSELF: ENROLL

Find a class, workshop, or conference to attend using one of the following suggestions. Enroll today.

HOW TO FIND A WORKSHOP OR CONFERENCE

★ Check out your local college or university. Many teaching schools have annual children's literature conferences that highlight local authors. They may also offer noncredit adult education courses.

★ Call the local school system for noncredit adult education classes being offered in your area.

★ Look in the May issue of *Writer's Digest* magazine. It lists a multitude of writers conferences. (That one in Maui looks pretty interesting!)

★ *The Writer's Essential Desk Reference*, edited by Glenda Tennant Neff, offers lists of writers colonies, workshops, and writing programs. Many books for writers offer similar lists.

★ Join the Society of Children's Book Writers and Illustrators or check out their Web site for updates on conferences. They have excellent local and national conferences.

Collaborate With a Friend

Some people find the prospect of developing their ideas so daunting that they need a little help. If you're that kind of writer, try hooking up with somebody. It doesn't need to be a friend, just someone who shares your desire to write. We were mere acquaintances when we began collaborating in 1986, but we've become great friends since then.

We've been very lucky and have made successful careers by collaborating so, of course, we are advocates of working with a partner. Pairing up with a buddy allows you to share the creative process as well as the secretarial chores. By bouncing ideas off each other, the chances are you'll be rewarded by even better ideas. If you're thinking about working with a partner, keep the following in mind:

1. Determine the division of labor. This will help avoid disagreements as the piece progresses. Who will prepare the manuscripts? Who will pay the postage? (We take turns and share the costs.)

2. Determine how money earned will be divided (it might be wise to draw up an informal agreement). We split everything fifty-fifty, which is spelled out in our book contracts.

3. Start small. Instead of saying, "Let's write together for the rest of our lives," try saying, "Lets write one story together and see how it goes." If you don't feel comfortable, you can always work independently on your next story.

4. Don't feel that every story must be a collaborative effort. Both of us have written stories on our own, even though we continue to write stories as a team.

5. If you don't feel comfortable writing with a partner, consider a writing buddy. This is someone who simply calls you to ask how your writing is going. Or you could try making writing dates with a friend. Agree to meet someplace to write for a certain period of time. Make it fun places like a playground, park, new café, or delicious restaurant. If your friend doesn't show up, it doesn't matter. Since you have scheduled that time to write, sit down and write! (But please remember to leave a good tip if you are taking up space in a café or restaurant.)

One of the easiest ways to find a writing buddy is to hook up with people at conferences and workshops. Many people like to extend a workshop's benefits by finding a partner willing to continue working on the skills covered in the class. Of course, we hooked up by talking about our secret desire to write. You might be surprised how many of your acquaintances share your goal of publishing for children. Just asking a few questions might put you in touch with a writing partner.

TRY IT YOURSELF: COLLABORATE

1. Locate a writing buddy. Try writing a story together.
2. Make a writing date with a friend. Agree to meet at a certain place and time. Then go there. Even if your friend doesn't show up, sit down and write.

Join a Writers Group

A writing critique group is one of the most beneficial tools available to writers. A critique group is a cadre of writers who meet periodically to help each other grow as writers. The old saying "It's hard to see the trees for the forest" can be true with our writing. Sometimes we are so close to our own writing that we're unable to see obvious imperfections. A critique group can help. Responses made by other writers during a critique session provide different ways of looking at your writing.

While it's always nice to hear that our writing pieces are great, it's the suggestions and comments about specific areas of weaknesses and strengths that help writers improve their art. Critique groups serve many purposes.

★ They help you assess ideas.

★ They help you improve writing skills.

★ They help you read more critically.

★ They motivate your writing, since you know you have to share something at the next meeting.

★ They provide a support group for dissemination of publishing news.

★ They provide a support group for sharing tales of woe about rejections and (hopefully) sharing the thrill of success.

FINDING THE PERFECT GROUP FOR YOU

★ Start with your local library. Does your librarian know of a critique group? Perhaps there is one that meets right in the library.

★ The same is true for bookstores. Many sponsor writing groups and host the critique sessions right in the store.

★ If there is a university or college nearby, check with the English department. Could they put you in touch with a local writers group?

★ Contact your local chapter of the Society of Children's Book Writers and Illustrators (SCBWI). When Debbie moved to Chicago she was able to join a critique group months before she even relocated. It made moving a little less scary to know she already had a support network waiting for her. If you can't find a local chapter, contact the international chapter of the SCBWI. They can put you in contact with members in your area.

★ If you can't locate a critique group in your area, don't fret. We had the same problem in Lexington, Kentucky, when we first started writing. We solved that problem by starting our own critique group. Since then, our original three members have swelled to more than twenty. That group grew by word of mouth, but you could also advertise at the local library, bookstore, or college.

The focus of critique groups may vary. Be sure to find a group that benefits you. There are three main reasons writing groups meet.

1. **To critique.** This kind of group spends the majority of the meeting reading and offering suggestions to writers.

2. **To share.** This group is more interested in sharing as a form of publishing. While some critiquing may occur, it is usually less thorough.

3. **To socialize.** Writing can be very lonely, so some writers meet just to socialize and share information about the writing life.

If you're looking for hard-core critiquing, you will be frustrated if you join a group primarily interested in socializing. If you aren't ready for in-depth critiques of your work, you will feel uncomfortable in a group that seriously analyzes participant's work. That's why it's important for you to know the focus of a critique group before joining it.

Forming your own critique group of trusted writing acquaintances could be the perfect way to keep your writing moving. When planning your own critique group, give some thought to how the sessions will be conducted. Will it be to critique? Socialize? A little of both? If you decide your group will primarily focus on critiquing, here are some helpful guidelines that will make each session more productive.

1. Define the focus of your group. During critique sessions, bring photocopies of a short sample of your recent work. Make enough copies for each member. Try to keep the sample under five pages, double- or triple-spaced. If you bring longer pieces, members won't have time to give it a thorough reading, and you'll end up with a less helpful critique.

2. Don't qualify your writing sample with any comments or explanations unless you want the group to focus on specific problems you are having. Otherwise, let your writing speak for itself. You can discuss your intentions after the group has responded to the writing. Keep in mind that you won't be able to qualify your writing to those big-time New York editors, either. Critique groups work, especially when writers are trying to prepare a manuscript for the critical eyes of editors. But if your purpose is to share your writing as a form of publishing and you would rather not have your piece critiqued, let the members know before you read your piece. This way they don't spend valuable time providing suggestions that you don't intend to consider.

3. Read your writing sample to the group members.

TRY IT YOURSELF: WRITERS GROUPS

1. Locate a local critique group and attend a meeting. It's natural to feel a little shy at first so you don't have to say a word if you don't feel like it, but do go and see what they're like.
2. If there isn't a group available, start one!

4. After reading, go to the snack table or play with the cats while the members silently reread your piece and jot down comments and suggestions.

5. When critiquing others' pieces, comment on specific areas. If a passage is good, say *why* it is good. This helps writers define and repeat their successes. Comment on sections that need spicing up and suggest improvements for unclear passages. In other words, try to figure out how the writing could be made better. Be sure to use positive comments for how writers might implement your suggestions. The purpose is to help writers improve—not destroy their egos! The chart below clarifies the difference between helpful and hurtful comments.

HELPFUL VS. HURTFUL COMMENTS

Helpful Critiquing Comments	Hurtful Critiquing Comments
I like the way you . . .	This isn't any good.
This part is effectively written because . . .	This will never sell.
Another way you could say this is . . .	This part made no sense.
Have you thought about trying . . .	You should start over.
Could this part be expanded by . . .	You haven't told the story.
Maybe you could try showing what happens by . . .	This was too preachy.

6. Once members have finished their individual silent critiques, take turns talking to the writer about the suggestions and comments. It's always tempting for the writer to jump in and explain his or her thinking behind the writing. Better to stay quiet and let the members finish their responses. If you aren't going to listen to what the group has to say, you are wasting your time—and theirs. It doesn't help to be defensive. In the end, the decision to change your story is your business. But while you're at a critique group meeting, listen to all the suggestions. The comments that annoy you the most may be on target.

7. After everyone has responded, the writer and members are welcome to have an open dialogue. But don't talk too long—others are waiting to have their pieces critiqued.

8. Finally, you may not have a piece ready to share. Don't let that keep you from attending and critiquing other writers' pieces. Critiquing helps you become a better writer, too.

Editorial comments and suggestions provided by members of a critique group might seem overwhelming at first. Remember, the purpose of

CRITIQUE CHART			
Strengths	**Areas for Improvement**	**Suggestions**	**Ideas**

critiquing is to identify places in your writing that need to be made stronger. That can be hard to take at first. When Marcia gets home from a critique session, she makes a chart with four columns like the one above to deal with comments.

She carefully analyzes the various responses made by the group members and jots down all the strengths mentioned. These are important. She wants to make sure to repeat and build on her strengths. Then, she notes suggested areas for improvement. Next to that, she briefly lists the suggestions made by critique group members. Finally, she brainstorms strategies for implementing the suggestions to improve weak areas while building on her strengths. She works on this chart a little bit at a time over the course of several days. Waiting serves two purposes:

1. Allows her creative muse to dig deeper for ideas.
2. Allows the sting of critiquing to fade!

Read a Classic

"I wish I could write a book like that." Debbie says that after reading almost any book. If you say that, too, then reading may serve as a big

TRY IT YOURSELF: READ A CLASSIC

1. Read a classic work recommended by your librarian.
2. Read an entire book of popular poetry for children.
3. Look for books similar to an idea you have. Read them.

motivator to keep your writing flowing. Read and get inspired.

It's important to sample many different types of writing. If you write fiction, don't limit yourself to reading only prose. Read poetry as well. You say you are not a poet and never hope to be a poet. That's fine, but still read poetry. Read it and let the beauty of the language sink into your brain. Your writing will reflect the experience whether you realize it or not. If you are a poetry writer, read nonfiction and fiction and listen to the cadence of the sentences. Nonfiction readers will learn a great deal from noticing the way fiction writers show plot and characters in action.

Don't forget to read works similar to what you have in mind. It will give you an idea of what has been done and what worked well. It will also let you know what to avoid.

Review the Previous Day's Work

Have you ever tried to hop over a creek? Did you stand at the edge and then spring effortlessly across? Of course not. You probably backtracked, ran a few paces, and then jumped. Those few running steps helped you build momentum. You can do the same with your writing.

When you sit down at the computer to begin your writing day, take a few moments to backtrack; read over your notes and at least the last page of your previous day's work. It will help you remember your voice and plot. Some writers even post a sign summarizing their plot to keep it foremost in their minds. We also make notes on our manuscripts with suggestions for what might happen next to help us get started on the next day's work. These provide us with those few running paces needed to leap onto a fresh page.

TRY IT YOURSELF: REVIEW

Today when you sit down to write, reread the previous day's work to get your mind back into the story.

Write a Letter to Your Audience

Having trouble getting your idea onto the paper? Try writing a note to your audience to see if it helps. Here's an example:

Dear Reader,

    I'm having a lot of difficulty saying what I want to say. What I'm trying to tell you is that the girl in my story is twelve years old. Her parents have just died, and she's been sent to live with Aunt Eugene and Uncle Dallas. They are wonderful people and my girl character loves them very much. Unfortunately, Aunt Eugene is not well and requires a doctor's care, which is hard to come by when no one seems to be able to find much work, including Uncle Dallas. My girl character is willing to help. That's why she eagerly carries a violin case into town for her uncle, just as he asked her to do. It seems like a strange request, but my character does it without question. When she drops the case by accident, everything becomes crystal clear. She has been breaking the law by helping sell moonshine. What should she do? Can she continue to help Uncle Dallas break the law and help Aunt Eugene?

Do you get the idea? Writing to your audience will help you get a handle on how to proceed with your story. You may even stumble upon an idea you never thought of before.

TRY IT YOURSELF: WRITE A LETTER

Select a story idea and write a letter to your readers telling them what you want to say.

Keep an Open Mind

Often we get so determined that our story must be a certain way that we're not open to new ideas offered to us by editors or well-meaning critique group members. In fact, we're so blinded by our original plan

TRY IT YOURSELF: KEEP AN OPEN MIND

1. Ask someone to read your work. Listen to his suggestions with an open mind, and write them down. Then put them away for at least two days. Take them out and look at the suggestions with an open mind. Are any of them worthwhile?

2. Try what John Steinbeck did as he wrote *East of Eden*. As you write, keep a journal. It could just be notes in the margins of your writing. Jot down any new ideas or personal reactions you might have had. Even if they don't fit into your writing plan, analyze each new idea as a potential cure for ailing writing.

we're not even open to our own brainstorms. Those new ideas added to your original might just be the spark needed to propel your writing to new heights—even if it means starting over and taking your story, poem, or article in a new direction. Pay attention to those unexpected sparks.

One of the best ways to encourage new ideas and directions for your writing is to keep a log or journal. Acknowledge new and different ideas by jotting them down. Write your sparks right on your manuscript-in-progress if you don't want to keep a separate journal. Don't negate them just because they don't fit into your plan. Some of those ideas might be the thing needed to freshen up your pieces. The important thing to remember is that new ideas, wherever they come from, are a gift not to be ignored. Keep an open mind and consider these gifts seriously.

Set Attainable Goals

Highly effective people set goals. Not only that, they review and revise their goals on a regular basis. Setting writing goals for yourself can help keep your writing energized. Of course, these goals must be ones that you have control over. For instance, Debbie's goal for the week we were writing this chapter was to finish chapter 3 in a story she's writing called "Whistler's Stump." That's a great example of a realistic, attainable goal. Don't set yourself up for failure by deciding you will complete a piece in a week or sell a book during the month of December. After all, you really can't control the market, and writing an entire piece during a busy month may be impossible.

You can keep your writing career moving by setting daily, weekly, monthly, and yearly goals for yourself. These goals will help you stay focused—especially if you write them down and display them close to your writing.

TRY IT YOURSELF: SET GOALS

1. Make two goals for this week, two more for the month, and two more for the year.
2. Assess your goals from activity one. Are your goals something you have control over?

Summary

Dedication, determination, and discipline are the fuel needed to keep your writing career moving. Having a writing buddy, belonging to a critique group, and going to writing conferences can help when you feel like you have writer's block. Writing letters to your audience, setting realistic goals, and reviewing the previous day's work can also get your writing engine sparked and ready to roll.

Remember, There really is no such thing as writer's block. There are only writers who are blocking their own success. Don't be your own roadblock. Get out of the way and write!

A LEAP OF FAITH

In this book we've discussed many strategies to generate ideas. Hopefully you've jotted down notes and thoughts as you worked your way through *Story Sparkers*. But what happens next? It's time to take that giant leap of faith and get started!

In this chapter we'll discuss everything you'll need to start shaping your favorite ideas into complete writing pieces. We'll consider strategies for assessing all of the ideas you've worked on so far to determine the brightest ones worth developing. After that, we'll put all the pieces together.

Here are some things we'll touch upon.

> **Claiming Your Personal Writing Space**
> **Finding Time to Write**
> **Assessing Your Ideas**
> **Jumping In**
> **Manuscript Preparation Hints**
> **Keeping Up With It All**

Castles, Gazebos, and Mudrooms

So, you have pages and pages of ideas. You've evaluated those ideas and selected at least one you want to pursue. Now comes the writing. But, before you begin shaping that great idea, you need to establish a time and place.

Don't decide to write on the kitchen table during the day while the kids are in school. That will mean your daily efforts will be wiped off by midafternoon so your family can prepare their evening meal. Eventually you'll give up because your family's meal takes precedence, and it's too much hassle to move things back and forth.

Saying you'll write in bed before you snuggle in for the night usually doesn't work, either. Chances are, you'll fall asleep before the words make it to the paper, and you'll end up with ink all over your pillowcase!

Believing you can write in the family room with the television blaring is a mistake, too. Distractions win out and your writing will go unfinished.

You must find a place and time to devote entirely to your writing. It doesn't have to be a castle or a fully furnished office. It doesn't have to mean an eight-hour day. But it does need to be defined for you, and more importantly, for your family and friends.

The first thing you must do is make a commitment. Tell yourself you're a writer, and believe it. It wouldn't hurt to make a sign and hang it beside your desk: *I AM A WRITER*. Then, make your family and friends believe it, too. Devoting a specific place and time to your writing sends a loud message to your family and friends: You are serious about your writing. Joel Strangis told us that when he goes upstairs to write, he tells his family he is going upstairs to work. That clearly shows his writing is serious business, not just a hobby.

Isolating a space just for writing lets family, friends, and your creative voice know that writing is important. The space you design should be for your use only. Be selfish. Sharing your computer with the kids won't work. Their homework, games, and Internet searches will squeeze out your writing time.

What little space you can claim as your own, do it. Don't worry. You won't have to build an addition to your home (unless, of course, you really want to). Debbie's dream is to someday have a gazebo-like garden room in which to work, but she also wants a mountain retreat with a babbling brook running beside it. If she waits until she gets that ideal setting, she won't get much accomplished.

Writing requires minimal equipment and space. Eileen Spinelli told us she first solved her space problem by claiming a tiny mudroom. It wasn't much, but it was hers, and with a large family that included another writer, it was exactly what she needed. Later, she "ousted the Honda from the garage and used that." She has also used a living room

TRY IT YOURSELF: CREATE A WRITING SPACE

1. Locate a place to claim as your writing space. This is one time when it's OK to be selfish!
2. Furnish your writing space with all the tools you need to write.
3. Put a sign over your writing space that says in bold letters, "I AM A WRITER."
4. Buy a really cool pen and journal or notebook. Take them with you wherever you go.

---

corner and the basement. Now she has a bright room all to herself.

Debbie converted her living room into an office, and Marcia claimed half of a spare bedroom. Margaret Mitchell wrote *Gone With the Wind* on a tiny desk in a small corner of her two-room flat. Your space doesn't have to be a castle, but it does need to be yours.

Look around your home. Is there a corner nobody uses? Clear it out for your writing. A spare bedroom? Take it. Having your own space devoted to writing serves many purposes.

* It allows you to organize your writing tools in a manner that supports your creative mind.
* You don't have to waste precious time setting up your space.
* It sends a loud message to your family that writing is serious business.
* It keeps your efforts focused on developing ideas rather than cleaning up.
* It allows you to shut the rest of the world out so you can concentrate on the ideas in front of you.

Our offices often look like a cyclone hit them when we're working on a story, which is all of the time. Clearing away the paper piles every few hours would restrict us from meeting deadlines. Debbie's office also has the look of a day care center, since her youngest child plays beside her while she writes. If she had to clean up the toys and the papers in addition to making dinner, somebody would end up going hungry.

Once you've claimed your space, furnish it with the essential tools of writing: desk, chair, paper, pens. Don't skimp if you can afford it. Buy that expensive pen you always wanted. If you enjoy the way it feels as you cover the page with words, you'll be more tempted to use it. The same goes for paper. If you don't have a computer, think about getting one. Computers are great creative tools. Word-processing programs make revising and editing as easy as pressing a few keys. Not only will a computer help you craft your ideas into completed pieces, it will also provide the clean, crisp printouts needed to send editors.

Golden Opportunities

Time is the most important commodity for a writer. So many responsibilities fill our days. Perhaps we should look at all our distractions as blessings—those same distractions provide us with additional fodder for writing. But the bottom line is you have to make the time to write if you plan to succeed. If you don't set aside time for developing your ideas, you won't ever get anything written.

How do you make time in an already too-full schedule? Here are a few suggestions.

Keep handy whatever method you've chosen for storing ideas. It's amazing the time you have to write when you're stuck in traffic or how sitting in the dentist chair can give you an idea. Marcia takes her journal everywhere, including restaurants, theaters, and the veterinarian's office. Debbie sticks a notepad and paper in her pocket when she goes for hikes in the woods. It's because we are all so busy that we must take advantage of the little bits of time we have here and there.

Perhaps you think you can't concentrate unless you have huge expanses of time in front of you. Hogwash. You can train yourself to do just about anything. According to an article in *Publishers Weekly*, J.K. Rowling got the idea for her best-selling Harry Potter series during a long train trip. Later, she developed her ideas while sitting in a café as her daughter napped beside her. Marcia wrote *Godzilla Ate My Homework* while her husband took a nap during their summer vacation. Let's face it: We can all make excuses, but if we want to succeed, we have to actually do the work. And if we want to succeed badly enough we will find the time—even if it's scribbling away while sitting on the toilet!

There are those that suggest you should schedule a specific time for your daily writing. Not only does this ensure your writing time, it also encourages your creative energy to habitually ignite during those set times. It makes sense. If you get in the habit of writing from 5:00 to 6:00 every morning, after awhile your creative muse will expect it just like your stomach expects to be fed at noon. So by all means, if you have the kind of schedule that allows you to write the same time every day, do it! If, on the other hand, you're like some of us whose schedules are ruled by other jobs, soccer games, ballet recitals, and travel, allotting the same time every day to your writing may be impossible. Don't be discouraged. Most of us fall into this category. Instead of writing the same time every day, try writing for the same *amount* of time each day. Instead of saying you'll write for two hours after dinner, the goal of writing two hours a day. Whenever you can, squeeze it in.

Two hours! Who has two free hours a day? Your day may already be packed with families, jobs, household chores, and television. Debbie couldn't do it all, so she rarely watches television. Marcia still teaches, so her schedule is packed, too. So let's be realistic. Maybe you can't give your writing two hours a day. Then start small. Dedicate ten or fifteen minutes a day to your writing and gradually increase it. Try the following suggestions to find those precious minutes in an already full day.

* Get up thirty minutes earlier every morning and use that time to write. You're fresher in the morning and you'll start the day successfully.
* Put a journal by your bed and write just a few words before going to sleep. Those gauzy twilight moments between being awake and falling asleep can be the most creative. If your creative muse kicks into gear as you fall asleep or wake up, be ready to write down those inspirational gifts.
* Keep a journal by your bed to jot down dreams. Some dreams can become unique sources of inspiration. If it happens to you, write it down before you forget. Don't wait until morning. It'll be too late.
* Always carry writing materials with you. Write while you're waiting to pick up the car pool; jot down ideas during red lights; scribble notes between appointments.
* Use your lunch breaks for writing. We started our writing career by writing during our twenty-minute teachers' lunch break.
* Eliminate two television shows from your viewing week. Use the extra time to write.
* Try using a minicassette recorder to capture precious ideas while driving or taking your daily walk.

Another way to increase the time you write is to schedule amounts of writing to complete instead of scheduling time to devote to writing. So if time increments make you freak out, challenge yourself to write a chapter, page, or even a paragraph a day. Remember: A page a day adds up to 365 pages by the end of the year.

TRY IT YOURSELF: FIND TIME TO WRITE

1. Develop a writing schedule. You don't have to keep it up for the rest of your life. This is just to get you started. Set aside a certain time or amount of time to write every day, then stick to it.
2. Commit to writing a certain amount each day. A paragraph, page, chapter, or even a sentence a day will get your ideas down on paper.

Panning for Gold: Choosing the Ideas to Pursue

Maybe you've looked over your ideas and thought, "These are all stupid!" Don't be so hard on yourself. Some of the simplest ideas can make the best-received stories. Look at the Caldecott Award–winning book by David Shannon, *No, David*. It is based on a simple idea, but something every child can enjoy. Ideas can be simple, just as long as you're not talking down to kids.

Maybe you've looked over your ideas and thought, "Wow. These are all great. I could write a book about every idea." If that's you, we're jealous. The truth is, not every idea is a good one. But don't be discouraged. We all come up with stinky ideas. Generating writing ideas is like panning for gold. The more rocks and mud you sift through, the more likely you are to find a speck of glittering gold. That's why the brainstorming phase is so important. You may have pages of muck, but don't worry. Buried within those pages are bound to be sparkles! Use the following strategies to find the gold in your pages of ideas.

★ Avoid ideas that are meant to teach. Didactic stories, articles, and poems with morals were popular years ago, but not today. It's OK to make a point, but any teaching must be subtle.

★ Look for ideas that are child-centered. Kids care about pets, families, and friendships. They don't typically worry about finances and long-term goal setting.

★ Make sure story conflicts can be solved by your kid character. Kids don't want to read a story where a teacher saves the day.

★ Search for ideas that appeal to adults as well as children, especially if you're planning to write a picture book or nonfiction book. It's true these books are intended for young children, but remember that adults are the ones who buy the books—and often must read and reread the stories to their children. Make sure the idea is appealing to the adult reader, too.

★ Shy away from making inanimate objects "human." Making a stapler come to life in a fresh and believable way is difficult to do.

★ Be careful if your idea features talking animals. Anthropomorphic stories are difficult to write without resorting to clichés. Some editors will not even look at this type of story.

★ Look for ideas that can be developed into a whole story without relying on the aid of pictures. Illustrations enhance your meaning, but the words must stand on their own.

★ Be careful if your idea includes rhyme. Many editors frown at submissions that rhyme because they are very difficult to do well.

★ Beware of clichéd ideas. Clichés aren't necessarily bad, in fact, they may be good ideas—so good that they've been done so often they've become old. Check your ideas against our favorite clichés in the sidebar below.

★ Jot down your favorite idea and think on it for a few days. Debbie thought about *Cherokee Sister* for two years before she began writing it. Are you still excited about your idea after a few days? Has the story started to write itself in your head? Can you not

OUR FAVORITE CLICHÉS

Ideas So Good They've Been Done to Death!

★ The too-little elf (or any creature) that somehow makes everything all right.

★ The rabbit with ears too big (or any character that's different) that no one likes until he saves the day.

★ The plain caterpillar that turns into a lovely butterfly or the ugly duckling that turns into a swan. (Hans Christian Andersen already did this one.)

★ There's no place like home. (L. Frank Baum did this in *The Wizard of Oz*.)

★ It was all a dream or a game. (Maurice Sendak did the dream in *Where the Wild Things Are*, and he's a tough act to follow.)

★ Anthropomorphized animals like Sally Squirrel and Bobby Beaver.

★ The creature (or object like in Watty Piper's *The Little Engine That Could*) that works hard and achieves success.

★ Stories involving a creature trying to be different than nature intended. Usually he finds out that being different wasn't all it was cracked up to be.

★ The scrawny Christmas tree that no one wanted that somehow saves Christmas. Of course, this could be a pumpkin for Halloween.

wait to write down the words? If you are not excited about your story, probably no one else will be either.

★ Highlight ideas that children would find interesting. If you're not sure, talk to a children's librarian or find a group of kids to interview. What do they think of your favorite ideas? Do they think children would be interested? (Keep in mind that these "test" children will like you and are therefore biased. Family and friends are not always your best critics, either. They may be afraid to hurt your feelings—or they may be too harsh!)

★ Check out the library to see if other books have been done that are similar to your favorite ideas. Browsing, a helpful librarian, and *Children's Books in Print* are all good ways to see what is already available. If you find books just like the one you had in mind, you need to give your idea a different slant. If your idea is very different, consider that it might be too different for the market.

★ Consider what it might take to develop your favorite ideas. Ideas that require lengthy development may be better suited for the adult market. Ideas that require little development may be better suited for a magazine article or poem.

★ Search for ideas that have something important at stake. If there's nothing important at stake, many readers won't invest the time to read your piece.

★ If your favorite idea is nonfiction, do research on your subject. Jot down notes and put them away. When you come back to them are you still excited by your idea?

★ If you envision your favorite idea as a picture book, consider the possible illustrations. Are there enough scene changes to support at least fourteen illustrations?

★ If you have an idea for a series, keep in mind that a series is rarely published by a first-time writer. Concentrate on one story and make it the best you can. Then you and your editor can decide if your idea can support a series.

★ Most children's stories incorporate dialogue. Is there room for dialogue in your idea?

★ Mom doesn't wear an apron anymore, and Dad doesn't always wear a suit. Be careful of stereotypes in your story ideas.

★ If you've sorted through your ideas and listed a few that you're feeling great about, keep reading. We'll tell you what to do next!

After you've found your golden idea, carefully nurture it with the five-step writing process we discussed earlier: thinking, writing, rewriting, editing, and publishing. When you've accomplished the monumental task of completing a story, don't forget to congratulate yourself. Go out to dinner or treat yourself to a bubble bath. You have done something most people only dream about. Take a break, because the next step is going to keep you busy.

Jump In!

Great. You've found a sparkling gem amidst all the ideas this book has encouraged you to brainstorm. Now what?

It's time to do what you've dreamed about: Write.

Beginnings are exciting. The potential of a new piece is inspiring but also a little frightening. Many writers, when preparing to embark on a new adventure, suddenly find themselves full of anxiety. What if they can't make it work? What if the idea is terrible? What if . . . ?

"What if" is a powerful phrase. Don't let it sabotage your dream.

If you're still feeling doubtful, turn to Appendix G, and find the planner that best suits your writing style and idea. Use it to organize your thoughts and give your writing direction. When you find holes in your plan, head for the library and research. Collect descriptions, ideas, and scenes in your journal. Then head back to your personal writing space and get ready to jump in.

Preparing Manuscripts

Before you start your draft, consider how the completed piece should look on the paper. This is especially important if you plan to submit your work for possible publication.

Use good quality paper, twenty pound or better. Format the page with an inch margin on each side and an inch and a half at the bottom. Each page should have your name and the story name at the top left-hand corner with page numbers on the right-hand side. The first page will be a little different. It will have no page number and the top left-hand corner will look like this:

Your name
Address
Phone number

Your first page will also look different because the title is centered halfway down the page. If you are writing a novel or chapter book, each chapter will start a new page. Never staple or paper clip your manuscript.

Entire books have been written about the correct way to submit a manuscript for publication. When we began writing an invaluable tool was the *Children's Writer's and Illustrator's Market*, which gives the correct form and helps with submission suggestions. The Society of Children's Book Writers and Illustrators (SCBWI) also puts out helpful publications in addition to their newsletter.

Most authors include a cover letter when they submit a manuscript to a publisher. A cover letter lets the editor know at a glance what you are sending. The first paragraph tells a bit about the book, trying to sound as enticing as possible. The second paragraph tells about you as a professional writer. If you don't have any publishing credits, leave off the second paragraph unless your job is something that relates to your story. Don't tell the editor that your children love your story. That will mark you as an amateur, which perhaps you are, but they don't need to know that.

A plain $10'' \times 14''$ manila envelope is fine for sending in your manuscript. Address it to a specific editor. Do a little research to find the right house and editor to submit your work to. Do this by observing the type of books different publishing houses put out and which one might like what you do. Look in *Children's Writer's and Illustrator's Market* or SCBWI publications to select possible publishers. When you send in your story, include a self-addressed stamped envelope (SASE) for the editor's response. Some people tell editors to discard their manuscript if they don't want to publish it. This may save you a few dollars in postage, but it also may send an unintentional message that you don't care much about your work.

Some writers find that including a self-addressed stamped postcard (SASP) with each submission helps them verify that their piece has been received. The postcard simply needs to read, "We have received your manuscript, *The Best Story Ever*, and will consider it for publication as soon as possible." When you receive the card back from the editor, you know that your piece has been received and opened and is in the process of being considered for publication. Be aware that some editors ignore the postcard, choosing not to return it to you until they have considered the manuscript and made their final decision.

After you've submitted your work you can't do much except forget it for a while. The best solution is to simply start another story.

After four to six months, it's time to check on your manuscript. If you haven't heard anything, it's fine to send a status query letter with a self-addressed stamped postcard. Be positive in your letter. Say something like, "I'm delighted you are still interested in my novel, Best Story

Ever, which I submitted on April 12, 2000. I hope to hear from you soon." The back of your postcard could look like the following.

_____We are still considering your story, Best Story Ever.

_____We are no longer considering your story and will
return it shortly.

DON'T KNOW WHAT'S GOOD PUBLISHING COMPANY

If wonder of all wonders happens and you get that call from an editor saying he would like to publish your book, don't go crazy. Take down all the information including how much the advance will be, what your royalty percentage will be, and if the publisher has considered an illustrator yet. Get the editor's phone number and ask to return his call when you've had a chance to consider the offer. Keep in mind that it is an offer and you can negotiate. You might want to call an agent or run to the bookstore to read up on contracts. Even though contracts can be a tremendous headache, take a few minutes out to celebrate. You did it! It is possible!

Keeping Up With It All

When those rejection letters start rolling in (and they probably will), it will be difficult to stay motivated. That's why having a support group or writing buddy can be beneficial.

You can also expect to get confused unless you have a system for keeping track of your submissions. Without one, you may make the mistake of sending an editor the same story twice or losing track of where the story is altogether.

We have several different handy-dandy systems to keep up with our submissions. We found three to be extremely helpful for different reasons.

The "Individual Manuscript Record" allows you to easily follow the history of a single piece. Whether it's a query with an outline or a completed piece, you can locate the status of each submission at a particular time by noting when you receive the SASP (self-addressed stamped postcard, if you send one) or a response to your submission. See a sample of this form on page 184.

The "Publisher Record" provides insight into how long it takes a particular publisher to respond and what types of responses the editor typically sends. If a certain editor always sends you a handwritten rejection with comments, this is a publisher you want to keep working with. If, on the other hand, you receive only form rejections from a certain editor, you may want to discontinue submitting to that publisher. We avoid submitting to some houses because their response time has been consistently slow. The "Publisher Record" also discourages you from making the mistake of sending more than one manuscript to a publisher at the same time. See a sample of this form on page 185.

The "At-a-Glance Record" lets you verify the status of all your submissions at once. By glancing at this one record, you can tell which submissions are still out, which SASP have been returned verifying receipt of your submission, and which pieces you need to continue marketing. See a sample of this form on page 186.

If you are like Marcia, you'll want all this information at your fingertips. Marcia found that one computer spreadsheet lets her easily access the same information as the three recordkeeping forms. Using a computer spreadsheet allows you to sort data by manuscript title, submission date, response date, or by publisher.

You may decide that using one simple record-keeping sheet will benefit you the most at this particular time. Maybe you feel more comfortable designing your own by combining information from all three and saving them as a computer spreadsheet. Just be sure to develop a personal record-keeping system that will help you keep up with each of your writing pieces.

TRY IT YOURSELF: KEEP UP WITH IT ALL

Review the record-keeping charts on page 184–186. Which will work for you? Start a folder or dedicate a computer file today. Each time you finish a story and submit it to a publisher, fill out a record form.

Summary

We hope *Story Sparkers* helps you ignite your own story sparks that are capable of turning into full-fledged stories, articles, and poems. Use the list below put it all together, and embark on your own writing journey.

We'll see you in the bookstores!

PUT IT ALL TOGETHER

★   Decide the most appropriate genre for you by using the exercises in chapter 1.

★   Generate ideas using the exercises in chapters 2 and 3.

★   Focus your ideas by reviewing the elements of writing and fundamental writing tools in chapters 4 and 5.

★   Sculpt your ideas with the tools in chapter 6.

★   Organize your writing using the planners in chapter 7.

★   Stay motivated and disciplined using the suggestions from chapter 8.

★   Take your writing seriously by determining your writing time and place after reading chapter 9.

★   Evaluate and select your favorite ideas using the pointers in chapter 9.

★   **Now . . . start writing!**

INDIVIDUAL MANUSCRIPT RECORD

Title:			Manuscript type:		
Intended Age or Grade Level	Proposal ❑		Complete ❑		Length

Publisher	Editor	Date Sent	SASP Return	Date of Response	Comments

Publishing company_____

Address_____

City/state/zip_____

Telephone_____

Manuscript title	Editor	Query or completed	Date sent	SASP Return	Date of Response	Comments

AT·A·GLANCE RECORD

Manuscript title	Editor	Query or completed	Date sent	SASP Return	Date of Response	Comments

APPENDIX A: AWARDS AND HONORS

NCTE Award for Excellence in Poetry for Children: Presented every three years by the National Council of Teachers of English recognizing a poet's body of work.

Boston Globe-Horn Book Award: Winners and Honor Books including fiction and nonfiction.

Caldecott Medal Award: Presented by the Association for Library Serivce to Children, a division of American Library Association, to the illustrator of the best picture book.

Claudia Lewis Award: Given by the Children's Book Committee at Bank Street College for the best poetry book of the year.

Coretta Scott King Award: Presented annually to an author and illustrator of African descent.

Flora Stieglitz Straus Award: Given by the Children's Book Committee at Bank Street College for nonfiction writing that gives a positive and realistic portrayal of real-world problems.

Golden Kite Award: Given by the Society of Children's Book Writers and Illustrators.

Hans Christian Andersen Medal Award: Offered every two years by the International Board on Books for Young People to an author and an illustrator who are judged to have made a lasting contribution to literature for young adults and children.

Josette Frank Award: Given by the Children's Book Committee at Bank Street College for fiction writing that gives a positive and realistic portrayal of real-world problems

The Irma S. and James H. Black Award: Given each spring for a book for young children that displays excellence for both illustrations and writing. Presented by the Bank Street College of Education.

Newbery Medal Award: Goes to the book selected as the best contribution to American children's literature in the United States. Given by the Association for Library Service to Children, a divison of the America Library Association.

Michael L. Printz Award: Awarded for excellence in literature for young adults.

Paul A. Witty Short Story Award: Given to the best short story appearing for the first time in a young children's periodical. Selected by the International Reading Association.

Work-in-Process Grants: The Society of Children's Book Writers and Illustrators sponsors grants in five categories to aid writers in completing manuscripts. The categories are: general work-in-progress grant, contemporary novel grant, nonfiction research grant, grant for an unpublished author's work, and a picture-book grant.

APPENDIX B: ORGANIZATIONS

American Library Association, 50 E. Huron, Chicago, IL 60611. (800) 545-2433.

Bank Street College of Education, 610 W. 112th St., New York, NY 10025. (212) 222-6700.

International Board on Books for Young People, Nonnenweg 12, Postfach, CH-4003 Basel, Switzerland. +4161-272 29 17.

International Reading Association, 800 Barksdale Rd., P.O. Box 8139, Newark, DE 19714-8139. (302) 731-1600.

Society of Children's Book Writers and Illustrators, 8271 Beverly Blvd., Los Angeles, CA 90048. (323) 782-1010.

APPENDIX C: BOOKS

Adams, Kathleen. *Journal to the Self*. New York: Warner Books, 1990.

Ballenger, Bruce, and Barry Lane. *Discovering the Writer Within*. Cincinnati: Writer's Digest Books, 1989.

Bernays, Anne, and Pamela Painter. *What If?* New York: HarperPerennial, 1990.

Bickham, Jack M. *Setting.* Cincinnati: Writer's Digest Books, 1994.

Card, Orson Scott. *Characters and Viewpoints.* Cincinnati: Writer's Digest Books, 1988.

Cook, Marshall. *Freeing Your Creativity.* Cincinnati: Writer's Digest Books, 1992.

————. *How to Write with the Skill of a Master and the Genius of a Child.* Cincinnati: Writer's Digest Books, 1992.

Dibell, Ansen. *Plot.* Cincinnati: Writer's Digest Books, 1988.

Dils, Tracey E. *You Can Write Children's Books.* Cincinnati: Writer's Digest Books, 1998.

Edelstein, Scott. *The Writer's Book of Checklists.* Cincinnati: Writer's Digest Books, 1991.

Goldberg, Natalie. *Wild Mind.* New York: Bantam Books, 1990.

Goldberg, Natalie. *Writing Down The Bones.* Boston: Shambala Publications, Inc., 1986.

Johnson, Kathryn Lee, ed. *Writing With Authors Kids Love!* Prufrock Press, Texas, 1998.

Knight, Damon. *Creating Short Fiction.* Cincinnati: Writer's Digest Books, 1981.

Lamott, Anne. *Bird by Bird.* New York: Pantheon Books, 1994.

Mogilner, Alijandra. *Children's Writer's Word Book.* Cincinnati: Writer's Digest Books, 1992.

Neff, Glenda Tennant. *The Writer's Essential Desk Reference,* 2d ed. Cincinnati: Writer's Digest Books, 1996.

Noble, William. *Conflict, Action and Suspense.* Cincinnati: Writer's Digest Books, 1994.

Novakovich, Josip. *Fiction Writer's Workshop.* Cincinnati: Story Press, 1995.

Olmstead, Robert. *Elements of the Writing Craft.* Cincinnati: Story Press, 1997.

Peck, Robert Newton. *Fiction Is Folks.* Cincinnati: Writer's Digest Books, 1983.

Pope, Alice, ed. *Children's Writer's and Illustrator's Market,* Cincinnati: Writer's Digest Books, (published annually).

Rico, Gabriele Lusser. *Writing the Natural Way.* Los Angeles: J.P. Tarcher, Inc., 1983.

Seuling, Barbara. *How to Write a Children's Book and Get It Published.* New York: Macmillan, 1984.

Smith, Michael C., and Suzanne Greenberg. *Everyday Creative Writing.* Chicago: NTC Publishing Group, 1996.

Tobias, Ronald B. *20 Master Plots.* Cincinnati: Writer's Digest Books, 1993.

APPENDIX D: PUBLICATIONS

Children's Book Insider, P.O. Box 1030, Fairplay, CO 80440-1030. (800) 807-1916.

The Horn Book Magazine, 11 Beacon St., Suite 1000, Boston, MA 02108.

Riverbank Review of Books for Young Readers, University of St. Thomas, 1000 LaSalle Ave., MOH-217, Minneapolis, MN 55403.

Writer's Digest, F&W Publications, 1507 Dana Ave., Cincinnati, Ohio 45207.

APPENDIX E: WEB SITES

Author Illustrator Source: http://www.author-illustr-source.com/. A national annotated listing of published writers and artists who make school visits and professional development presentations.

Children's Book Insider: http://www.write4kids.com/aboutcbi.html. A subscription newsletter for children's writers and illustrators.

Children's Literature Web Guide: http://www.acs.ucalgary.ca/~dkbr own/index.html. Provides links to articles and writing resources for writers, parents, and teachers.

Inkspot.com: http://www.inkspot.com/. A comprehensive sight featuring the online magazine, *Inklings*, articles, marketing information, and links to helpful sights.

PublishersWeekly.com: http://www.publishersweekly.com/. An online site for the magazine covering all aspects of publishing.

The Society of Children's Book Writers and Illustrators: http:// www.scbwi.org. Focusing on children's writers and illustrators, this site includes feature articles from national and regional SCBWI bulletins, and information about awards, grants and conferences.

APPENDIX F: WRITER'S LINGO

Advance on royalties: amount paid to the author before royalties are accrued (usually received upon signing of contract and completion of manuscript).

Chapter hook: cliff hanger at the end of a chapter enticing the reader to turn the page.

Contract: legal paper agreeing to the publisher's terms.

Cover letter: a brief synopsis of work with the writer's qualifications.

Editor: person who reads manuscripts and considers them for publication.

Genre: category of writing such as fairy tale, mystery, poetry, biography.

Manuscript: paper copy of a story or article.

Motif: repeated story element.

Multiple submissions: sending identical manuscripts to several publishers at the same time.

Muse: source of inspiration.

Point of view: point or identity of narration.

Postcard (return): a self-addressed stamped postcard enclosed with a manuscript. The postcard can be returned by the editor on receipt of the manuscript.

Publisher: person who turns the manuscript into a book.

Rejection: letter rejecting your work for publication.

Royalty: percentage based on the sales of a book paid to a writer for the right to publisher's work.

SASE: self-addressed stamped envelope; used for return of manuscript.

Show, don't tell: phrase used to remind writers to show what is happening rather than just telling.

Slush pile: all the unsolicited manuscripts sent to publishers.

Style: writer's unique use of sentence structure, word choice, and syntax.

Theme: underlying focus of your story.

Voice: distinctive style or writing personality.

SUBTOPIC OUTLINE

Title:

One-line summary:

Subtopic 1	Subtopic 2	Subtopic 3	Subtopic 4

CHAPTER OR SECTION SYNOPSES

Title:

Chapter or Section	One-line Summary:
1	
2	
3	
4	
5	
6	
7	
8	
9	

Title:

One-line summary:

Character
Who is this story
about?

Setting
Where and when
does this story
happen?

Conflict
What problem must
the character solve?

Climax
What crisis forces
the character to
either succeed or
fail?

Resolution
How has the
character changed
or grown?

Plot
What happens in
this story? Why and
how do they
happen?

NONFICTION ELEMENTS

Title:

One-line summary:

Beginning
How can I hook the reader?

Middle
How can I bring this to life
for the reader?

Ending
What do I want to make sure
the reader has learned?

Title:

One-line summary:

Conflict/Complications	Character(s) Reaction	Effect of Reaction
(the problem and complications)	(what the character does)	(what happens as a result)

FICTION·BOOK PLANNER: STORY ELEMENTS

Title:

Plot: One-line summary telling what the book is about

Theme: Word or phrase that tells the deeper, worldly truth that the book is really about

Main character(s) and brief personality description

Antagonist: A brief personality description of the adversary of the main character

Conflict: What is at stake?

Complications that thicken the plot

Setting of place and time

Climax: Briefly describe the turning point or moment of no return.

Conclusion: Where will the characters be at the end? What has changed?

Chapter #	Main Events	How Events Relate to the Theme

CRITIQUE CHART

Strengths	Areas for Improvement	Suggestions	Ideas

INDIVIDUAL MANUSCRIPT RECORD

Title: **Manuscript type:**

Intended Age or Grade Level   Proposal ❑   Complete ❑   Length

Publisher	Editor	Date Sent	SASP Return	Date of Response	Comments

PUBLISHER RECORD

Publishing company_____

Address_____

City/state/zip_____

Telephone_____

Manuscript title	Editor	Query or completed	Date sent	SASP Return	Date of Response	Comments

Manuscript title	Editor	Query or completed	Date sent	SASP Return	Date of Response	Comments

APPENDIX H: 100 QUICK STORY SPARKS

Have a few minutes to have some fun? Pick a number and start sparking.

1. Make a web of the thing you fear the most. Use the web to write a story.
2. List what you like best about the Christmas holiday. Use your list to create a picture book.
3. Write a conversation between two friends who are having a fight. This might be the beginning, the middle, or the ending of a great story.
4. Write a letter to your fourth-grade teacher.
5. Remember the day you learned to ride a bike.
6. What if the teachers at your school weren't quite normal? What if they really did have eyes in the back of their heads?
7. Compare a chocolate cake to failure.
8. Set your clock for three minutes. Close your eyes and think of the first grade. While your eyes are closed, use a marker to doodle.
9. Play music that you can't stand. Now pretend you are a sixth grader whose parents love this music. They play it when they pick you up from school, they play it when you have friends over—and they play it loud. How do you cope?
10. Describe the meanest person you have ever known. How did the person get that way?
11. Make a web of what the year 2020 will be like. Use your web to write a poem.
12. Go to a park and find a seat on a bench. Sit for a few minutes and soak in the atmosphere. Now write.
13. Write a dialogue between Santa Claus and the Easter Bunny.
14. Go to the library and browse in the adult nonfiction section. Pick a book on a topic that has always interested you. Learn all you can about that topic. Write a nonfiction article about it for a magazine.
15. What did you want to be when you were five years old?
16. What if your pet really could talk? What would it say to you? What would you say back?
17. Pick up a magazine. Pretend the first child you see in the magazine has a secret. What is it?
18. Compare a tornado to school.
19. Pretend your father is a gangster during Prohibition. What is your life like?
20. Look at an atlas and pick a city you'd like to visit. Write about it.
21. Ask a five-year-old what you should write a story about, then write it.

22. Write a recipe for the most delicious concoction you can think of. Don't worry if it doesn't make sense, just have fun writing it. Now pretend you are a kid trying to sell that concoction.

23. Write a letter to your best friend in elementary school. You don't have to send it.

24. Find something you have had since childhood. How did you get it? How would you feel if someone broke it or it was lost?

25. Go see a movie. Now, rewrite the story so it has a different ending.

26. Go someplace you've never been before. Write a nonfiction piece about it.

27. Draw a picture of the perfect person. Now, write about that person. They may not be so perfect after all!

28. What is the happiest thing that ever happened to you when you were a child?

29. Make up a stupid song about toenails.

30. Eat something new. Pretend you are a kid who has to eat it. How are you going to get out of it? Try making it into a picture book.

31. Pretend you broke both of your legs right before field day. What happens? Who wins the race you were going to win?

32. Make an outline for a story about meeting your hero. Is it easy to meet him? Does he even notice you?

33. Make a list of fifty wishes. What would happen if one of your wishes came true?

34. What if two people on the same elevator each made a wish at the exact same time? What if the wishes came true, but they accidentally got each other's wishes?

35. Pick your favorite sport. Write a story about a kid who badly wants to play that sport, but can't because of a handicap.

36. Make a web of brave things.

37. List twenty different ways for a second grader to get into trouble.

38. Write a conversation between a cat and a dog.

39. Look out your window and imagine that you see a stranger walk by. Where is he going? What is his name? Make up a character sketch about this stranger.

40. Make a time line for a fictional historical character.

41. What if the British had won the American Revolution? What would our country be like today?

42. Describe a nervous person without actually saying he is nervous. Now, try to figure out why he is nervous.

43. Compare homework to sunshine. Now give that homework to a fictional character. What happens?

44. Set your timer for five minutes and close your eyes. Pretend you are in second grade. Can you smell paste or the kid at the desk beside you? Doodle on a sheet of paper with a green marker while you remember.

45. Play some music that you love. Now, pretend you created that music. What was your life like?

46. What if your parents moved you to a foreign country? How would you feel?

47. Write a letter to your best friend on planet Earth from your home on Pluto.

48. Make up a sad song about growing up.

49. Write a paragraph about the hardest part about growing up.

50. Pretend you are a famous movie star, age fourteen. You get a letter from a kid in trouble. What would you do?

51. Make up an imaginary friend for a three-year-old.

52. Write a story about a five-year-old child's birthday party where everything doesn't go exactly as planned.

53. Pretend you are twelve. Make a list of the things you love and another of the things you hate.

54. Finish this sentence. The thing I like to do most is. . . .

55. What if your favorite thing came to life?

56. Make up a classroom list, complete with teacher. What is life like in that classroom?

57. Write a page about the most perfect vacation you can think of. Now, have something go very wrong.

58. Pretend you find a real genie's lamp. What would you wish for? Write three wishes and what happens when you make the first wish.

59. Rewrite the story of *The Three Bears* with the bears as the good guys.

60. Pick your favorite character from a movie or book. Now, give them a new name and story.

61. What if you woke up one morning and you were in a fairy tale? Which would it be? How could you get back to reality?

62. In your grandmother's trunk there is a treasure map. What is it to?

63. Make a web of friends you have known. Pick one to write a letter to.

64. List scary monsters. Pick one to write about.

65. Write a conversation between a mouse and a mousetrap.

66. Pretend it is winter and you are looking out your bedroom window. That is all you ever see because you are not allowed to go out. Why not?

67. Make an outline for a chapter book about a first fishing trip.

68. What if the sky was purple instead of blue?

69. Your mom thinks all girls should learn ballet, but you have two left feet. How do you feel?

70. Describe being lost.

71. Make up a happy song about growing up.

72. Make up a television show that a child would love.

73. Pretend you are an alien and this is your first Halloween.

74. Read the newspaper and clip out columns of interest to you. Follow up on at least one idea, and write a query letter to an editor asking if she'd be interested in a 700-word article about your subject.

75. You are the only kid in first grade who has not lost a tooth. Write a paragraph about it.

76. Write a dialogue between a grouchy old man and a tiny little kitten.

77. You found a tea party hat, complete with plumage, lace, and satin flowers. Now you must find who it belongs to. Write about your adventure in at least two pages.

78. In your Aunt Agatha's old house, something strange happens when the grandfather clock strikes three in the morning. What happens?

79. Make a web about school. Is there one thing that interests you more than others? Write about it.

80. Go to a place near water. Perhaps it is a waterfall, a stream, or even an aquarium. Sit and watch the water for a while. What were you thinking about?

81. Your parents went on a day trip and didn't come back. You were left in charge of your six-year-old brother. What will you do?

82. Write a picture book about Santa's wicked cousin.

83. Pretend you can fly.

84. Write a conversation between a scrawny kid and her sibling.

85. You are a drummer in the Revolutionary War. Write a letter to your parents.

86. Pretend you are wearing pointy-toed boots. Who are you and where do you live?

87. What if the school bully wanted to be your friend?

88. It really bothers you when people pops bubbles with their gum. Your science teacher does it all the time. One day she pops one too many. What happens?

89. Your dad finally takes you fishing, and it's not what you thought it would be like. Write your mom a note.

90. Your mom helps you fly a kite. Write a magazine story about it.

91. You found twenty dollars. No one claimed it so you decided to spend

it. Now, two days later someone says it was her money. What should you do?

92. Ask a ten-year-old what you should write about, then do it.

93. You are going to Egypt. It is exciting until your parents disappear into a pyramid.

94. Your father is the blacksmith for a Wild West town. When he falls ill you have to take over even though you're only ten.

95. Imagine you are four years old. Look at your surroundings. What do you want to know about?

96. How does a computer work? Research the answer and write a nonfiction article about it.

97. What if you suddenly acquired superpowers?

98. Write about your special place.

99. Make an outline of a story where the electricity goes out. You are home alone with one flashlight. The batteries are so weak that the flashlight goes out. You are in total darkness.

100. It's your birthday and there's only one thing you want. What is it?

INDEX

A

Across the Wide and Lonesome Prairie, 94
Adjectives, 129
Advance on royalties, 191
Adventures of the Bailey School Kids series, 1-2, 54-55
Adverbs, 127
Agents, reading fees, 113
Alice on the Outside, 79
Amelia Bedelia stories, 14
American Cheerleader magazine, 9
American Girls series, 15, 69
American Library Association, 11, 16, 188
Analogies, 105
Anecdotal experiences, 102
Animals
    anthropomorphized, 177, 178
    See also Pets
Are You There God? It's Me, Margaret, 16
Armageddon Summer, 66
Association of Library Service to Children
    Caldecott Medal, 11-13, 187
    Newbery Medal, 16-17, 187-188
At-a-glance record, 182, 186, 203
Awards
    list of, 187-188
    See also Caldecott Medal books; Newbery Medal books; Printz Award

B

Baby Born, 84
Babybug magazine, 9
Bailey City Monsters, 101
Bandage Bandits, The, 83
Bank Street College of Education, 188
Batbaby, 82
Bauer, Marion Dane, 9, 19, 63, 64, 72-73
Baum, L. Frank, 178
Beginning
    of fiction plot, 99
    of nonfiction book, 102-104
Bein' With You This Way, 79
Beliefs, 47-48
Best Christmas Pageant Ever, The, 125

Big Moon Torilla, 75
Birdsong, 86
Blue and the Gray, The, 74
Blume, Judy, 16
Boo Who? A Spooky Lift-the-Flap Book, 78
Book doctors, 113
Bookstores, 84
Boring, Mel, 113
Bowie, C.W., 81
Bowman-Kruhm, Mary, 81
Boyds Mills Press, 87
Boys' Life magazine, 9
Bradby, Marie, 9, 73
Brady, Marie, 71
Brain, left vs. right, 29-30
Brainstorming, 31-33, 83, 108, 134
Bride of Frankenstein Doesn't Bake Cookies, 34
Bright and Early Thursday Evening: A Tangled Tale, 86
Brill, Marlene Targ, 74
Bulla, Clyde Robert, 74, 94
Bunting, Eve, 64, 74-75
Busy Toes, 80
Butterfly House, 64
By the Great Horn Spoon, 57

C

Cache of Jewels and Other Collective Nouns, A, 77
Caldecott Medal books, 11-13, 187
Calliope magazine, 9
Capriotti, Diana, 87
Chalk Box Kid, The, 74
Chapter books, 14-15, 23
Chapter hook, 191
Chapter synopses
    fiction-book planner for, 148
    form, 199
    planner, 194
    See also Section synopses
Characters
    in chapter books, 14
    child protagonist, 97
    create-a-character form, 92-93
    dialogue and, 136
    as fiction elements, 90-91

likeable, 27
main, shoes of, 59-60
in middle-grade novels, 15
personality of, 124
plot and, 63
rewriting and, 111
types of, 90
Charlotte's Web, 15
Cherokee Sister, 16, 59, 177
Chicago Manual of Style, The, 115
Chickens Aren't the Only Ones, 77
Children
    as inspiration, 82
    listening to, 22
    questions by, 38
    reading and, 22, 150
    testing ideas with, 177
    what they care about, 68, 176
    world of, 94
    writing "down" to, 26
Children's Book Insider, 190-191
Children's Books in Print, 103, 177
Children's literature, selection of, 23-25
Children's market, 8. *See also* Markets
Children's Writer's and Illustrator's Market, 116, 180
Children's Writer's Word Book, 150
Chocolate, Debbi, 70, 75
Classic books, 165-166
Cleary, Beverly, 15, 69
Clichés, 10, 177-178
Climax, story, 97-98
Cobblestone magazine, 9, 70
Collaboration, 160-161
Coming Through the Blizzard, 65
Commander Toad books, 66
Computer
    idea files, 6
    playing games at, 84
    record-keeping spreadsheet, 182
    writing at, 36, 174
Conflict, 95-97
Conrad, Pam, 59, 98
Contract, 191
Conversation
    in story. *See* Dialogue
    overhearing, for ideas, 42-43
Cover letter, 191
Coville, Bruce, 66
Cow Who Wouldn't Come Down, The, 78
Cowley, Joy, 75
Crash, 16
Critique chart, 165, 200

Critique group, 110, 112, 161-165
    finding, 162
    forming, 163
    helpful vs. hurtful comments, 164
    revision and, 112
Curriculum-based ideas, 69-71
Cursing, 16

D
da Vinci, Leonardo, 7, 58
Dadey, Debbie, 15, 16, 34, 39, 48, 54-55, 59, 69, 101, 155, 177
Daughter of Liberty: A True Story of the American Revolution, 82
Dean, Tonya, 87
Dear America series, 69, 94
Delivery, 84
Dialogue, 135-137
    as conversation, 135
    in easy readers, 14
    in good books, 27
    ideas and, 43-44
    in middle-grade novels, 15
    punctuation with, 136
    readability and, 135
    tags, 136
    writing effective, 136
Dibell, Ansen, 99
Didactic writing, 134
Distractions, 157-158
Dlouhy, Caitlyn, 87-88
Dolphin Log magazine, 9, 70
Don't Look and It Won't Hurt, 81
Doodling, 58-59
Drafting, 109-110
Dreams, 87

E
Early Winter, An, 72
Easy readers, 13-14, 23
Edelstein, Scott, 116
Edison, Thomas Alva, 109
Editing, 114-115
Editors, 191
    advice from, 87-88
    magazine, 8
    picture book, 11
    role in revision, 112
Elements of Style, The, 115
Elephant Upstairs, 83
Emperor and the Kite, The, 87
Encyclopedia Brown series, 16
Ending
    of fiction plot, 99-101

of nonfiction book, 105
Erickson, John R., 150
Excuses, 157-158
Experiences, 77, 86-87
    anecdotal, 102
    ideas and, 64-66

F
Fact, startling statement of, 103-104
Family anecdotes, 83
Family Apart, A, 80
Fancy That, 78
Fantasy genre, 21
Farmers' Market, 78
Far North, 78
Fiction
    book planners, 146-149
    hooks in, 131-133
Fiction elements
    character, 90-91
    conflict, 95-97
    plot, 99-101
    resolution, 98-99
    setting, 91, 95
    story climax, 97-98
    See also Story elements
Fiction Is Folks, 90
Figurative language, 137-138
First-person point of view, 120-121
Fleischman, Paul, 20
Fleischman, Sid, 75-76
Folklore, 75
Follow in Their Footsteps, 85
Forced relationships, 53-55
Fourth Grade Rats, 83
Fox, Mem, 9, 76
Frankenstein Doesn't Plant Petunias,
    147-148
Free association, 78
Freedman, Russell, 19, 40
Freewriting, 35-36, 83
Frog and Toad books, 14

G
Genre, 191
    audiences and, 149-151
    choosing a, 20-21
    trends and, 21-22
    See also Markets
Ghost Canoe, 78
Gift story, 73
Goals, attainable, 168-169
Godzilla Ate My Homework,
    15, 52, 69, 174

Goldberg, Natalie, 35
Golden Kite Award, 187
Gone With the Wind, 173
Goosebumps series, 16, 68
Gordon Wilfred McDonald Partridge, 9
Grammar check, 115
Grand Escape, The, 80
Grandfather's Rock, 72, 84
Gregory, Kristiana, 94
Guideposts for Teens, 87

H
Hall, Jacque, 76
Hank the Cowdog series, 150
Happy Monster Day, 78
Harry Potter books, 15, 20, 174
Hatchet, 97
Haunting, The, 80
Heller, Ruth, 77
Henry Huggins, 15, 69
Henry's Awful Mistake, 83
Here and Then, 126
Herman, Charlotte, 64, 71, 77
Hershenhorn, Esther, 77
Hesse, Karen, 94
Hobbs, Will, 78
Holub, Joan, 78
Hooks
    chapter, 191
    fiction, 99, 131-133
    nonfiction, 132
    picture books, 132
Hopkins, Lee Bennett, 19
Hopscotch magazine, 9
Horn Book Magazine, The, 26, 190
House on Walenska Street, The, 71, 77
How to Hide a Crocodile and Other
    Reptiles, 77
How to Hide series, 77
How the Stars Fell Into the Sky: A
    Navajo Legend, 9, 68, 81
Howe, James, 150
Howliday Inn books, 150
How-to books, 105
Humor, 27, 75
Hyperion Books for Children, 88

I
I Have a Weird Brother Who Digested a
    Fly, 78
Idea box, 79
Idea envelope, 108
Ideas
    audiences and, 149-151

choosing among, 176
collecting, 6-7
editors' advice for, 87-88
from famous authors, 63-88
focusing, 89
generating, 31-61
organizing. *See* Organizing ideas
quick story sparks, 204-208
researching, 154
sculpting, 119-139
as starting point, 88
If I Were in Charge of the World and Other Worries: Poems for Children and their Parents, 20
If You Were Born a Kitten, 9, 19, 72
Illustrations
chapter books, 14
easy readers, 13
picture books, 10-11
See also Pictures
Imagery, 105
Imani in the Belly, 75
Individual manuscript record, 181, 184, 201
Inner City Mother Goose, The, 20
International Board on Books for Young People, 188
International Reading Association, 188
Internet research, 154
Interviews, 156
Island Magic, 84

J

Jacques, Brian, 146
Jalapeño Bagels, 86
Jim Ugly, 57
Johnson, Kay, 116
Johnson, Paul Brett, 9, 32, 63, 67, 78-79
Jones, Marcia Thornton, 15, 34, 48, 52, 54-55, 69, 71, 101
Journal
collecting ideas in, 6
daily, 73, 83
freewriting in, 36
next to bed, 175
Joyful Noise: Poems for Two Voices, 20
Kane, Thomas S., 115
Keynoter magazine, 9
Kids. *See* Children
King of the Kooties, 97
King, Stephen, 16
Knots in My Yo-Yo String, 19, 83

L

Lamott, Anne, 49-50
Language
figurative, 105, 137
fresh, 87
See also Word choice
Lawlor, Laurie, 51
Let Women Vote, 74
Letters
to audience, 167
cover, 191
fictional, 46
ideas and, 44-46
rejection, 181, 192
researching, 156
Lewis Hayden and the War Against Slavery, 19, 70, 84
Library research, 154-156
Lincoln: A Photobiography, 19
Lion to Guard Us, A, 74
Listening to kids, 22
List of events, 108
Listing ideas, 36-38
free form list, 37
organized list, 38, 143
Little Bear books, 9
Little Engine That Could, The, 178
Lobel, Arnold, 14
Long Way From Chicago: A Novel in Stories, A, 81-82
Longest Wait, The, 9, 71, 73
Lunch Money and Other Poems About School, 20
Lyon, George Ella, 9, 126

M

Magazine market, 8-9
Magazines
curriculum-based, 70
ideas from, 67, 83
researching, 155
titles, 25
Magic Tree House series, 15
Maniac Magee, 83
Manuscript
defined, 191
preparation, 179-181
submissions, 181-183, 191
Markets, 8-20
chapter books, 14-15
easy readers, 13-14
magazine, 8-9
middle-grade novels, 15-16

nonfiction, 19
picture books, 9-13
poetry and verse, 19-20
young-adult novels, 16, 19
See also Genres
Max Malone Makes a Million, 77
Maze, The, 78
Mazer, Harry, 81
Memories, 77, 86
early, 81
ideas and, 64-66
writing to remember, 71-72
Merriam, Eve, 20
Metaphors, 27, 137-138
Middle
of fiction plot, 99
of nonfiction book, 104-105
Middle-grade novels, 15
good stories for, 87
selection of, 24
Millie Cooper series, 77
Minarik, Else Holmelund, 9
Mitchell, Margaret, 173
Mogilner, Alijandra, 150
Monster, 19
More Than Anything Else, 73
Motif, 191
Mr. Persnickety and the Cat Lady, 67
Mrs. Wishy-Washy, 75
Multicultural genre, 21, 83, 86
Multiple submissions, 191
Mummies Don't Coach Softball, 155
Muse
defined, 192
musical, 60
Museum research, 155
Music From a Place Called Half Moon,
18, 81, 91
My Mom the Frog, 15
Myers, Walter Dean, 18, 19
Mystery genre, 21

N

Napping House, The, 86
Nate the Great books, 14
Naylor, Phyllis Reynolds, 79-80
Networking, 159
New Oxford Guide to Writing, The, 115
Newbery Medal books, 16-18, 187-188
Newspaper, ideas from, 66-67, 73-75, 80,
83
Night Before Easter, The, 86
Night of the Gargoyles, 74

Night Before Halloween, The, 86
Nikola-Lisa, W., 7, 64, 79
Nixon, Joan Lowery, 80
No, David, 176
Nonfiction
beginnings, 102-104
elements of, 101-105, 196
endings, 105
hooks in, 132
market, 19
middle of, 104-105
selection of books, 24-25
series, 69-70
North, Becky, 32
Nouns, 127-129
Novels
middle-grade, 15, 87
young-adult, 16, 19, 87

O

Objects, 77
Observation
of funny things, 75
ideas and, 79, 82
Old Dry Frye, 78
Old, Wendie, 80-81
Omniscient point of view
third-person, 121-122
third-person limited, 122
On the Day I Was Born, 75
On My Honor, 65, 72
One Hole in the Road, 64-65, 79
One-line summary, 133-134
1, 2, 3, Thanksgiving, 79
Open mind, 167-168
Organizations, list of, 188
Organizing
ideas. *See* Organizing ideas
information, 105
into scenes of action, 108
Organizing ideas, 141-152
fiction-book planners, 146-149
with lists, 143
outlines, 141-143
plot events, 146
section synopses, 144-145
story elements, 144-146
subtopics, 143
Osborne, Mary Pope, 15
Oughton, Jerrie, 9, 18, 67-68, 81, 91,
108, 110, 126
Out of the Dust, 94
Outlines

benefits of, 142
organizing ideas, 141-143
planning and, 108
restrictions of, 142
story element, 144
subtopics, 143
Owl Moon, 64, 87

P
Page quotas, 158-159
Parish, Peggy, 14
Paulson, Gary, 97
Peck, Richard, 81-82
Peck, Robert Newton, 90
Perelman, Helen, 88
Permission to fail, 156-157
Pet peeves, 51-52
Pet words, 111
Pets, 76
    cats, 79
    missing, 69
    See also Animals
Phrases, overheard, 82
Picture books, 9-13
    child protagonist in, 97
    hooks in, 132
    illustrations in, 10-11, 178
    length of, 10-11
    selection of, 23
Pictures
    ideas and, 50-51
    See also Illustrations
Pigman, The, 18
Piper, Watty, 178
Planners
    chapter or section synopses, 194
    fiction-book, 146-149, 198-199
    subtopic outline, 193
Planning
    with outline, 142
    in writing process, 107-108
Plants that Never Ever Bloom, 77
Plot
    character and, 63
    easy reader, 13-14
    events, 146, 197
    as fiction element, 99-101
    middle-grade novels, 15
    from newspaper stories, 80
    rewriting and, 111
    theme vs., 134
    young-adult novels, 16
Plot, 99

Poetry and verse
    market for, 19-20
    reading, 81
    rhythm in, 130-131
    selection of, 25
    See also Rhyming stories
Point of view
    defined, 191
    first-person, 120-121
    third-person, 121-123
Pope, Alice, 116
Possessions, 57-58
Postcard
    return, 192
    See also Self-addressed stamped post-card
Prairie Songs, 98
Prelutsky, Jack, 19
Prewriting, 107-109
Printz Award, 19, 188
Problem books, 16
Publisher
    defined, 192
    researching, 88
Publisher record, 181-182, 185, 202
Publishing, 115-116
Punctuation with dialogue, 136

Q
Quackenbush, Robert, 82-83
Questions
    engaging, 104
    as idea sparks, 38-39, 102
    "what if," 48-49, 66, 85
Quotas, page or word, 158-159

R
Ramona series, 15
Random House, 87
Rapunsel, 9
Rawlings, Marjorie Kinnan, 99
Reading, 22, 81, 150, 165-166
    aloud, 110
    for ideas, 52-53
Red-Eyed Tree Frog, 75
Redundancy, 111
Redwall, 146
Reference books, 188-190
Rejection letter, 181, 192
Relationships, forced, 53-55
Relaxation, 84
Research
    to enrich ideas, 154-156
    for ideas, 39-40

Internet, 154
interviews and letters, 156
magazines, 155
museum, 155
publishers, 88
Reviewing work, 166
Revision
    checklist, 112
    stage, 110
    See also Rewriting
Rewriting, 84-85, 110-114
Rhyming stories, 10. *See also* Poetry and
    verse
Rhythm, 129-131
Ribsy, 15
*Riverbank Review of Books for Young
    Readers*, 190
Robinson, Barbara, 125
Rowling, J.K., 15, 20, 174
Royalties
    advance on, 191
    defined, 192
Running for Our Lives, 85
Rynearson, Pat, 83

S

Scene descriptions, 102
Scenes of action, 108
Scheduling writing time, 174-176
School Library Journal, 26
Schoolyard chant, 83
Section synopses, 144-145
Section synopses planner, 194
Self-addressed stamped envelope,
    (SASE), 180, 192
Self-addressed stamped postcard,
    (SASP), 180-181, 192
Self-publishing, 116
Sendak, Maurice, 44, 178
Senses
    ideas and, 40-42
    setting and, 95
Series books
    curriculum-based, 69
    popularity of, 15
Setting, 27, 91, 95
Shannon, David, 176
Sharmat, Marjorie, 14
Shields, Carol Diggory, 20
Shiloh, 79, 150
Shoes, main character's, 59-60
Shoeshine Girl, 74

*Shooting Star: Annie Oakley, the Leg-
    end*, 9, 39
"Shotgun Cheatham's Last Night Above
    Ground", 81
Show, don't tell, 137, 192
Silverstein, She, 19
Similes, 27, 137-138
Simon and Schuster/Atheneum, 87
Singing Down the Rain, 75
Slam, 18
Slang, 115, 136
Slush pile, 192
Smells, 77
Smith, Robert Kimmel, 68
Sobol, Donald J., 16
Society of Children's Book Writers and
    Illustrators (SCBWI), 22, 180, 188,
    191
Sounds, ideas and, 75
Space Station Seventh Grade, 66
Sparkle words, 26-27
Spell check, 115
Spinelli, Eileen, 20, 65, 172
Spinelli, Jerry, 16, 19, 65, 66, 83-84
Stereotypes, ideas and, 80
Stiles, Martha Bennett, 84
Stine, R.L., 16, 68
Story climax, 97
Story elements, 90
    fiction-book planner for, 147, 198
    forms, 195, 198
    organizing ideas through, 144-146
    See also Fiction elements
Strangis, Joel, 19, 63, 70, 72, 84
Strays Like Us, 81
Strunk, William Jr., 15
Style, 123, 192
Subtopics
    organizing ideas with, 143
    outline planner, 193
Suen, Anastasia, 84-85
Summary, one-line, 133-134
Surprise for Mrs. Burns, 85
Suspense, 27
Sweet Strawberries, 79
Synopses, section, 144-145, 194

T

Tags, dialogue, 136
Take Me Out to the Airfield, 82
Take a Walk in Their Shoes, 85
Tales Twice Told, 116
Talking Lizard, The, 83

Theme, 134, 192
There's a Girl in My Hammerlock, 66
There Goes Lowell's Party, 77
Thinking
   small, 49-50
   in writing process, 107-109
Third-person point of view, 121-123
Time lines, 55-57
Time, scheduling writing, 174-176
Title file, 83
Toddler Two, 84-85
Tooth Tales From Around the World, 74
Trail of Tears: The Cherokee Journey From Home, The, 74
Traveling Cat, A, 9
Trends, 21-22, 88
Triplet Trouble series, 69
"Truth or Dare", 71
Turner, Glennette T., 85-86
Twelve Shots, 81
Two Slapstick Biographies, 82

V

Vampires Don't Wear Polka Dots, 2, 48-49
Vanity presses, 116
Verbs
   active vs. passive, 127
   choice of, 127
   present vs. past tense, 125-126
Verse. *See* Poetry and verse; Rhyming stories
Very Special Kwanzaa, A, 70, 75
Viorst, Judith, 20
Voice, 123-125
   defined, 192
   fresh, natural, 26

W

Walking, 84-85
Wall, The, 74-75
War in Georgia, The, 81, 126
War With Grandpa, The, 68
Web site
   authors', 154
   list of, 190-191
Webbing, 33-35
What Does the Rabbit Say?, 76
What if questions, 48-49, 66, 85
What's the Magic Word?, 78
When Mama Comes Home Tonight, 20
Where the Red Fern Grows, 150

Where the Wild Things Are, 44, 178
Whipping Boy, The, 57
White, E.B., 15, 115
Who Are You?, 80
Wild Minds, 35
Wilfrid Gordon McDonald Partridge, Whoever You Are, 76
Window Music, 84
Wing, Natasha, 86
Wirths, Claudine, 80
Wizard of Oz, The, 178
Wizard's Hall, 87
Wombat Divine, 76
Wood, Audrey, 86-87
Word choice, 125-129
   adjectives, 129
   adverbs, 128
   nouns, 127-129
   verbs, 125-127
   See also Language
Word quotas, 158-159
Work-in-process grants, 188
Workshops, 159-160
Wringer, 66, 83
Writer's block, 153
Writer's Book of Checklists, The, 116
Writer's Digest, 190
Writers group, 161-165. *See also* Critique group
Writing class, 159-160
Writing out of sequence, 156
Writing process
   drafting, 109-110
   editing, 114-115
   prewriting, 107-109
   publishing, 115-116
   rewriting, 110-114
   thinking, 107-109
Writing space, 171-174
Writing tools, 173-174

Y

Yearling, The, 98-99
Yolen, Jane, 64, 66, 87
Young-adult novels, 16, 19
   good stories for, 87
   selection of, 24

Z

Zelinsky, Paul, 9
Zillions: Consumer Reports for Kids magazine, 70
Zindel, Paul, 18